Conquering Inner Space

CONQUERING INNER SPACE

JOHN WARREN STEEN

BROADMAN PRESS
Nashville, Tennessee

422–240

DEWEY DECIMAL CLASSIFICATION: 248

Library of Congress catalog card number: 64–24024

Printed in the United States of America

1.5N66KSP

To

Dorothy Jean

Preface

PROJECT MERCURY reached a climax recently with astronaut Gordon Cooper's twenty-two orbits of the earth. Project Gemini has already been charted for a two-man capsule to rendezvous with an orbiting supply spacecraft. Then will come Project Apollo, which intends to send a full crew of astronauts to the moon in 1970. After a slow start, America is enjoying success in conquering outer space. In contrast, we have made little progress in conquering inner space.

You and I are living in the space "rage." Our government is spending millions of tax dollars for exploration, but many of us seem unwilling to expend fifteen minutes' worth of brain power in looking within. The great discoveries of the last half of the twentieth century need not be limited to outer space.

Perhaps you have realized the need for a great thrust forward in your own spiritual progress. You need to explore inner space. Maybe you are beginning to realize a drag from childishness or a loss of power because of unchanneled emotions. Now is the time for you to begin this journey of spiritual exploration.

Do not consider it impossible. Do not use age as an excuse. You can accomplish things regardless of your years. When I was only four-and-a-half-years old, I was able to do something that the grown-up people next door were not able to do. They were not able to get their little boy, my same age, to stop taking his bottle. Every morning he would come out to the sidewalk, warmed by the brilliant Mississippi sun, and lie down, still wearing his pajamas, to suck on his baby bottle. I laughed, poked fun, and ridiculed the child until he finally gave up the bottle. I found that you get something done by keeping at it.

With confidence, you can face the challenge of your soul's development. Astronaut John Glenn said to his minister, "I pray every day and not just when the chips are down." Such an attitude will bring real progress in the inner space race.

I have written these simple studies to indicate the adjustments you can make to the pressures and anxieties of the space age. You will find these thoughts expressed in the language of today but based on the teachings of the ancient Scriptures. Just because something is old does not mean that it is old-fashioned. Progress in the spiritual realm is not measured by distance but by depth. When you put these old ideas to work in your modern life, you will discover areas of Christian living as exciting as a new planet and as rewarding as a ticker-tape parade.

The discovery and exploration of inner space will not be easy. Some of us have become lost in the crowd. We have not discovered ourselves because we are conforming to outside demands, moving in any direction the crowd pushes. I heard a high school boy say, "I am exposed daily to the cliques in our schools—the little groups who keep to themselves, play 'follow-the-leader,' and have no initiative or will power." The conformist can never discover himself while still conforming.

When you begin individually the discovery of your inner resources, you will discover your own originality. This is not the nonconformity of the beatnik type nor of the switchblade gang. It is the natural individuality that the Creator intended you to have.

You can decide to be yourself, like young David did. He thought of battling Goliath, wearing the heavy armor which King Saul offered him. The king was reputed to be head and shoulders above all of his soldiers. When David tried on the armor, he looked like a turtle in a shell. He decided to be himself, and he discarded the ridiculous armor. He went into battle wearing his own loose-fitting shepherd's clothing and carrying his own familiar weapon, a slingshot. He could not fit into the mold of someone else.

When you become yourself, you will release the hero who is tied up within you. You will want to attempt something great. You will be like the young man who attends his first class in medical school. He vows, "I'll discover a cure that will make the world healthier." A young man at theological school says, "I'll always choose the right, and I'll transform the church." A new member, emerging from the waters of baptism, says, "I'll serve Christ all my life, regardless of the cost."

The people who will really bless the world in the space

age will be those who are truly themselves. They will have discovered the latent power in their lives, and they will channel that power into constructive use.

I hope that some who read these words will become the individuals God intended them to be. I hope that some David will refuse to accept the burdensome armor of anxious conformity. I hope that some reader with the determination of an Albert Schweitzer will direct his talents to thrill an unconcerned world. I hope that some young woman with the dedication and persistence of a Florence Nightingale will bless the world. I hope that some young man with the eloquence and compassion of George Truett will go forth to preach and to lead. I hope that some reader with the skill of Dr. William Wallace will also have his dedication of purpose for the cause of Christ.

I hope that some quiet "nobody" will recognize his own potentialities and become a "somebody" for God. I hope that someone, crippled physically or emotionally, will be able to accept his limitations with serenity. I hope that some misfit who has never found himself will become acquainted with what he really is and will cultivate this self-knowledge which can lead to a break-through in the soul's courageous adventure.

Contents

Contents

Conquering Inner Space

1
Roadblocks to Maturity

EVERY TIME you have dealings with people, you find that some of them are immature. In business or in church work, you discover stunted personalities and dwarfed souls. They are grown up physically, but they have refused to grow emotionally or spiritually.

What is immaturity? It is a board member pounding on the table, demanding his way of doing things. It is a woman of middle years, silly and giggling, because of too many martinis. It is a college student telling his parents what is wrong with them emotionally. It is a high school girl sulking and pouting over not getting a luxury she expected. It is a woman consulting a palmist or a horoscope for her orders of the day. It is a church member who objects to the picture of Jesus blessing the children of the world, because it might teach integration. It is a college trustee who wants to fire any professor who does not agree with his own theology. It is a Christian who has never given up the childish idea that God records every sin in a celestial ledger with indelible ink.

15

You can do something about immaturity, if you will.
You can recognize roadblocks to maturity in your own
life and set out on a program of clearance and progress.

I

One roadblock is delayed infancy. Why be an infant
when you can enjoy the fun of growing up? You should
continue to expand and grow. As your mind and body
develop, let your soul do likewise. If you have the temptation to loll about in religion's cradle, get out and start
exercising your soul.

When she was twenty-two years old, Sarah Flower had
an untroubled faith that had been nurtured by her devout
parents. But that year she met a boy, Robert Browning,
and he strongly influenced her life. Although he was only
fourteen years of age, he had read widely. He could discuss with her the ideas of the classic doubters and atheists.
Miss Flower became so disturbed in her own beliefs that
she wrote to her brother-in-law, a minister, these thoughts:
"And now as I sit and look up to the room in which I first
had existence and think of the mother who gave it . . . the
thought links itself with another—how much rather would
she I had never been, than to be what I now am."[1]

Her immature faith had been questioned. Yet Sarah
Flower worked through her doubts. She spent effort in
her patient search for a mature religion. Years later, she
wrote a great affirmation of her faith in the hymn, "Nearer,
My God, to Thee." Robert Browning likewise began to
hammer out a Christian faith, which still inspires the
reader of his enduring poems.

A mature religion never comes to you packaged and

polished and ready for consumption. Like the apple you find at the grocer's, it must be selected and paid for, washed and polished, before it is useful to you.

One of my teachers at the seminary told of an older teen-age girl who came to him for counseling. She was disturbed over the fact that she had just experienced a close relationship to God. It made her question a similar childish experience when she joined the church. The latter experience so overshadowed the earlier one that she tended to discount the earlier one. He said this to her: "You don't wear the same shoes now that you wore back then. Your foot has grown, and you need larger shoes; but that doesn't mean that you didn't need shoes back then. Your religious experience now is meaningful for you, but you should not let it cancel out your earlier experience. One suited your needs then; one suits your needs now."

A mature faith should be ever expanding and progressing, once the roadblock of cherished infancy is removed. It is regrettable that many people know nothing more of biblical faith than Noah's ark and Jacob's ladder, which they learned in the Beginner department of the Sunday school. After that period they stopped growing.

A grown person has gladly discarded the clothes he wore as a child. He has no interest in the infantile toys he once enjoyed. His mind has increased in every subject from geography to psychology. The only thing he holds on to is his childhood religion. With a sentimental impression of the simplicity of his childhood religion, he relinquishes that last of all. However, it is a roadblock that must be removed to achieve maturity.

You will be quick to remind me at this point of the

words of Jesus that "except ye . . . become as little children, ye shall not enter into the kingdom of heaven" (Matt. 18:3). Correct! And yet I am sure that our Lord would be the first to recognize the difference between a childish religion and a childlike faith. He was praising the purity and teachableness of a child. He was not praising the stubborn, infantile habits that need to be discarded for adult behavior.

The average person passes through two periods of religious development before he obtains a mature religion. One period is the late juvenile or early adolescent religion. It usually is an imitation of that of the parents, if both of them are in agreement. If parents have different beliefs, then it is imitative of the parent who has the most influence. Many well-meaning parents who are both of the same faith spend time and energy trying to root a docile, unquestioning belief in their child. They discourage the very qualities he will need in late teens and early adulthood. They squash independent judgment and spiritual discernment, which would enable the child later to cope with a world of question, despair, and doubt. The child's religion is largely a matter of habit, and he wonders why there is so little relation between it and everyday life.

Later in adolescence follows a second period. It is a reaction to the previous stages. The child begins to rebel and to renounce the traditional. He gets the idea that religion is bad medicine which his parents have been spoon-feeding him, and he begins to fight it. It is a period of self-assertion and reaction, and it occurs in many young people, in varying degrees.

After these periods, maturity becomes a possibility. The

young person finds that it is unrealistic to live as if there were no God. He soon tires of an endless search for pleasure. When he marries, becomes a parent, and realizes a responsibility to his mate and children, he recognizes his need for divine guidance and exemplary conduct. In this final period of maturing, the young adult takes the best features from the previous periods of docility and rebellion. He tailors these to fit his individual needs. His religion is now distinctively his own.

Another minister and I had just finished dinner with a doctor at the North Carolina Baptist Hospital. After we started home, the other man paid a high compliment to the physician's religion when he said the following: "That doctor has worked out a philosophy of religion that will fit in with his present life situation. He has not tried to make a childish religion fit, but he has built on it, so that now it is in harmony with the rest of his life. It has intelligence and depth."

His choice brings to mind the two lads in Sam Walter Foss's poem:

> A boy was born 'mid little things,
>   Between a little world and sky—
> And dreamed not of the cosmic rings
>   Round which the circling planets fly.
>
> He lived in little works and thoughts,
>   Where little ventures grow and plod,
> And paced and ploughed his little plots,
>   And prayed unto his little God.
>
> But as the mighty system grew,
>   His faith grew faint with many scars;

> The Cosmos widened in his view—
>   But God was lost among His stars.
>
> Another boy in lowly days,
>   As he, to little things was born,
> But gathered lore in woodland ways,
>   And from the glory of the morn.
>
> As wider skies broke on his view,
>   God greatened in his growing mind;
> Each year he dreamed his God anew,
>   And left his older God behind.
>
> He saw the boundless scheme dilate,
>   In star and blossom, sky and clod;
> And as the universe grew great,
>   He dreamed for it a greater God.[2]

II

Another roadblock is selfishness. This one is the largest impediment for many people.

Recently in a discussion group with college students, I asked them to name spontaneously some marks of immaturity. They indicated uncontrollable temper and irresponsibility, which they realized were both egocentric. Then they named selfishness. Next they mentioned being inconsiderate. Also listed as a sign of immaturity was the inability to face difficulties and to handle anxiety. They soon saw that selfishness was a basic factor in each of these traits of immaturity.

Maturation means a shifting of attention from self to others. A psychiatrist, Harry Stack Sullivan, defines adulthood as a time when one is able to establish relationships with others who are as significant as one's self. Mature people discard selfishness with childhood toys. They "will be quite sympathetically understanding of the limitations, interests, possibilities, anxieties, and so on of those among whom they move or with whom they deal."[3]

Selfishness makes a person sensitive and easily hurt. Have you ever seen a grown man get peeved because someone besides himself was selected as a deacon? Have you seen a grown woman pout because she did not have a place of honor on a church committee? It makes you ask, "How childish can people get?"

You expect a child to be self-centered, but you do not expect this attitude in an adult. The child thinks only of himself. He becomes naughty and refuses to co-operate with other children when he first meets them as playmates. He must learn their value by a gradual process. The youngster has an intense love for himself, and it is hard for him to learn to love anyone else with equal concern.

A seminary colleague, who now teaches at Vassar College, pointed out the self-centered religion of a child by examining his prayer life. The child thinks only of himself; in his immaturity he prays this prayer:

> Now *I* lay me down to sleep,
>   *I* pray the Lord *my* soul to keep.
> If *I* should die before *I* wake,
>   *I* pray the Lord *my* soul to take.

After he loses some of this childish self-interest, he can pray this prayer:

> Lord, help me live from day to day
> In such a self-forgetful way

That even when I kneel to pray
My prayer shall be for—Others.[4]

III

Another roadblock is a religion that stresses kind
thoughts but leaves out Christ. Like a department store
window at Christmas time, it is sentimental and attractive but shallow. It tells only a fragment of the story of
the cradle, cross, and crown.

The most mature religion is that which places Christ in
the center, so that in "all things he might have the pre-
eminence" (Col. 1:18). God came to us in history as a
man. In a way, this is the easiest way to picture God—in
the form of Jesus the Christ. Yet this is the most sublime
way. "God was in Christ, reconciling the world unto
himself" (2 Cor. 5:19). Jesus brought to this world the
grandest qualities and the purest life this world has ever
known. He continues to give the dynamic for living cou-
rageously. As one young adult stated it, "My religion is
more than just living out the principles of Christ; it is
attempting to live close to Christ."

The eminent psychologist of Harvard University, Gordon W. Allport, wrote a friend of mine in Louisville a
letter in which this statement of his belief appeared:

It seems to me that historic Christianity can be taken, not as
naturalistic nonsense, but as an expression, in the best ap-
proximate terms, of all experience that is most profound and
real to many human beings. It is as though mankind said to
itself, "With such a sublime life and teaching what else could
Christ have been excepting the Son of God? And how else
could man conceive of a God above life, a God in man, and
God moving dynamically through time, excepting in terms of

the Trinity?" I am saying that it seems to me that historic Christianity forms a perfect groundwork for mature religious thinking, and many mature people find it the best for their needs and mental powers.[5]

A mature religion is valuable in the way it meets modern life. It is able to meet the doubts, the frustrations, and the disappointments of life with the conquering message of Christ. It can reconcile itself with the findings of science and have a mighty impact on the morals of the world. It can change men to think of others more than of themselves. It can cause all Christians to think of the ethical implications of the gospel in terms of social action.

A mature religion is useful. It can help a person avoid a nervous breakdown, and it can aid in restoring mental health. It can help unite families that have been disrupted in their relationships. It can help in time of alarm.

A boy by the name of William was struck with infantile paralysis when he was very young. Through many months his mother continued to massage his legs in hope that he would walk again. After he took his first few steps, someone said to his mother, "Those massages worked miracles."

Then she replied, "So did my prayers."

The boy learned from his mother the meaning of prayer and about the courage that could be gained from Christ. He used that strength when he started mountain climbing to strengthen his legs. He was sensitive about his small legs, because the children laughed at them; but he climbed hills and mountains to strengthen them. He succeeded. Today there is nothing he had rather do than to climb mountains.

Once he was climbing on some treacherous rocks when they gave way. As he slipped, he grabbed a ledge above. He was left hanging by his fingers, two hundred feet above the nearest rocks. His fingers and arms went numb. Then the last words of his dying father came to him: "If I die, it will be glory. If I live, it will be grace." He knew that it would take God's grace for him ever to come out alive. He prayed for strength and courage.

God gave him both. He hung on until his friend had maneuvered around and found a toe hold for his feet. That night beside the embers of a campfire, he knelt down on some fir boughs and thanked God. That man today has a profession of great responsibilty. He did not select his religion because of its utilitarian value, but he found its usefulness beyond compare.

A faith that demolishes the roadblocks of infancy, selfishness, and shallowness will bless your life. You will never be satisfied that you have achieved a mature religion; like the aging apostle, you can say, "Not that I have already obtained, or am already made perfect: but I press on" (Phil. 3:12, ASV).

2

How to Love Yourself

YOUNG PEOPLE are very sensitive about their shortcomings. Pimply Pam envies the cover girl's glamor. Clumsy Carl dreams of becoming an athlete. Dull Dora would consider it a compliment to be called an egghead. Timid Ted is discontented as a follower. They, like many older Christians, have deep feelings of inferiority which keep them from living adequate Christian lives.

Jesus said, "Thou shalt love thy neighbour as thyself" (Matt 19:19). Have you ever stopped to think that you cannot properly love your neighbor until first you properly love yourself?

There is nothing wrong in taking an interest in yourself. I remember announcing to a college group that I would speak on the subject, "Is It Wrong to Love Yourself?" An attractive girl checked with me to be sure she understood correctly the time of the lecture. When the hour came, she was the first to arrive. This lovely blonde, with leadership potential, was interested in herself, and she wanted to find out if this concern was sinful.

We need to develop the same appreciation for ourselves that Christ has for us. He said, "Lay up for yourselves treasures in heaven" (Matt. 6:20). He meant that if you expect your soul to grow, you must be interested in it. He wants you to love yourself. The kind of self-love Christ recommends is not adoration but appreciation. It can be attained by a Christian who is interested enough to work at it.

I

In order to love yourself, discover yourself. The thrill of Columbus' sighting the new world or of John Glenn's gaining a new perspective of the world in vivid colors from outer space can be yours when you begin to discover yourself. Search the horizon of your personality for those strange motivations that make you act in your own distinctive way. Rise to inquiring heights to gain a perspective on your relation to the universe.

Many times a dream can tell you about yourself. While I was a student in the seminary, an old friend visited me overnight. I gave him my bed and slept on the floor; rather, I relaxed on the floor—there was little sleeping that night. Sometime before dawn I dropped off to sleep and dreamed of my friend. I saw myself angrily plunging a knife into him. Could such a profane thought originate within the sacred walls of the theological seminary? Could such a repugnant wish come from a Christian? Of course! When I admitted to myself that I was capable of having murderous thoughts, I came to know myself better. If I had refused to recognize these negative feelings, they could have become dangerous.

Daydreams are common in the life of a teen-ager. If a youth doesn't have some dreams, how is he going to have a dream to come true? Once a college student came to talk with me, much perturbed about his plans for graduate study. He was undecided about which field of study to pursue. He should have been thinking about his undergraduate work. Instead of listening to the professor's lecture, he would look out the window and daydream about a master's or doctor's degree. When he went to his room, he lay on his bunk daydreaming about his future popularity. What he was doing was failing in his school-work and escaping the reality of schedules and hard work.

Fear of parental disapproval causes some indecision. I have known young people to refuse to join a church. Typical is the case of a boy whose father is Catholic and whose mother is Protestant. The lad claims he is not convinced of the truth of either religion. Actually, he does not want the responsibility of deciding for one parent and against the other. The sooner he realizes this underlying motivation, the better off he will be, and the quicker he can make some decision about the important matter of church membership.

Rebellion against parents can likewise be an unrecognized motivation. A child in elementary school, a daughter of a Baptist minister, reported that she could no longer believe in God. This p.k. (preacher's kid) was a neglected child. She did not realize it, but she was using the only weapon she had at her disposal. She was rebelling against her father and his work which kept him from her. The father received some counseling help and began to show more interest in his daughter's activity. He took her to the library; he went swimming with her. Her disbelief evaporated like the dew on a June morning.

What you forget can tell you much about yourself. Have you ever forgotten an appointment? Chances are the appointment was with someone you found disagreeable. On the other hand, if you were invited to the White House for a meal with the President and his family, there is no possibility that you could forget this important occasion.

The mind plays some strange tricks. Slips of the tongue, procrastination, strange aches and pains, and pet patterns of speech can tell you much about yourself. Learning about yourself can be a fascinating discovery.

When you discover conflicting motivations and ideas, it might seem more confusing to know yourself. A poet with keen insight wrote the following words:

> Within my earthly temple there's a crowd;
> There's one of us that's humble, one that's proud,
> There's one that's broken-hearted for his sins,
> There's one that unrepentant sits and grins;
> There's one that loves his neighbor as himself,
> And one that cares for naught but fame and pelf.
> From much corroding care I should be free
> If I could once determine which is me.[1]

The only true way to discover yourself is from God's perspective. You can find yourself through the process of prayer, but you must learn to be yourself in prayer. Like the honest psalmist, you can say, "Search me, O God, and know my heart: try me, and know my thoughts: And see if there be any wicked way in me, and lead me in the way everlasting" (Psalm 139:23-24).

Like Job, whose prayers were filled with complaints

and even doubts, you can share your real self with God. Many times our prayers are superficial and fickle because we try to present to God a pretty picture of our personalities. After all, the Lord who knows all things knows the blackest thoughts of our hearts. We cannot escape from him, and we should not try. When we deal with him truthfully, he will bless us with the gift of self-discovery.

II

Before you can love yourself, you must accept yourself. You can be thankful that your fingerprint is different from that of anyone else. Similarly, you can be thankful that your personality is different from that of anyone else. What a dull world it would be if everyone were just alike. Accept the differences and be thankful for them.

Peter, James, and John were tremendously varied in their personalities. Each one understood Jesus and reacted to him in a different way. On one of the resurrection appearances, Peter asked Jesus about John. He received the following reprimand from his Lord: "What is that to thee? follow thou me" (John 21:22).

A salty old woman of the Beverly Hillbillies type made the following comment on personality differences: "Most folks are born to be like they are, and every one is a good specimen of the kind he is. Salt is awful if you expected it to be sugar, but it's just right if you're thinking of salt. I'd be awful, too, if folks expected me to be Jayne Mansfield, but I'm a perfect example of me."

I recall my own anxiety in attending my first minister's

meeting in a new town. I paused in the doorway and looked for some familiar face. There was not a person that I recognized. However, from across the room a stranger started smiling and came toward me with outstretched hand. I began to feel better. When he got to me, I introduced myself. "You're the wrong one," he said, and walked away muttering, "I thought you were the guest speaker."

To myself I thought, "I'm the right one but in the wrong place." We need to recognize our differences and distinctions from others, and we need to accept these.

Having respect for yourself is reasonable. The head psychiatrist at a large general hospital always asks this question of a patient at a staff conference: "What are your plans?" If the patient has not had enough respect for himself to start making some realisitic plans, this is automatically a sign that he needs more emotional treatment and care. If he has begun to plan ahead, this fact is one indication of his return to emotional stability.

When you accept yourself you will know your talents and use them. In a realistic appraisal of talents, the person of average mentality will not crave an executive position. The timid person will not expect to make a success of salesmanship. The person of a creative mind will throw it away if he enters on a dull, routine job which calls for no imagination. The person who properly loves himself will recognize his talents and will use them.

III

As you begin to love yourself, you will dedicate what you are. The college girl who showed such an interest in the lecture on self-love did not concentrate on her own looks and accomplishments. The last time I saw her was when I performed her wedding ceremony. She was beautiful and radiant, but she was not thinking about herself that day. Even though she had spent hours in preparing her makeup, her coiffure, and her pearl white satin wedding gown, she was thinking only of the young man she loved.

When Jesus visited the Temple as a lad of twelve, he was interested in himself. He knew that he needed to learn more. He was beginning to catch some predawn glow of the coming day of his service. Consequently, while others were searching the highway and town for him, he participated in a Temple discussion group, eager to use the opportunity for his vocational preparation.

It is not surprising that five-year-old Tommy asked his mother about the cross upon the church altar. Not satisfied with her answer, he said, "The T stands for Tommy." As he grows more mature his interpretation will become reversed, and he will think of the symbol as "the I crossed out."

You can have true respect and love for yourself when you understand that Christ valued you enough to die for you. Then you will be eager to dedicate yourself.

Lloyd Douglas reconstructs the story of Jesus' interview with surprised Zaccheus. "Come," said Jesus, "I am dining with you." Proud to be thus singled out, and yet amused at his self-invited guest, Zaccheus decided he would entertain the Carpenter in a manner fit for a king. In spite of his best efforts, he knew that the dinner was not much of a success. When the meal was over, he sent the servants from the room. Even with the servants present, Zaccheus had been uncomfortable. But now the atmosphere seemed intolerable. Slowly raising his head, he looked for the first time straight into the eyes of Jesus. The eyes held him fast. "My friend," Jesus said, "a great salvation has come to your house today."

The short, inferior man, who had used his financial talents to deprive and defraud, suddenly promised restitution to those he had wronged and pledged further gifts of charity for the poor. He was beginning to love his neighbor as himself. When Jesus asked the explanation of these strange actions, Zaccheus replied, "Good Master, I saw, mirrored in your eyes, the face of the Zaccheus I was meant to be!"

3

Doubt's Question Mark

HAVE YOU ever been out by a beautiful pond where fish were biting and discovered that you had brought no fishing tackle? When I was a lad I found myself in that predicament, but I tried bending a pin, putting a rolled up piece of bread on it for bait, and tying it on to a long willow switch. Needless to say, I caught nothing. But when I exchanged the pin for a sharp hook, even using bread for a bait, I began to catch some fish.

Sometimes we use the bent pin of blind acceptance, when we really need the sharp hook of doubt's question mark. Yes, the question catches many ideas and thoughts from the pool of knowledge. Socrates said, "The unexamined life is not worth living." Similarly, the unexamined spiritual life is not worth exercising.

Perhaps you have come up against the problem of doubt and have felt guilty. Maybe you have not realized that doubt is an almost universal experience. Sometimes, people are surprised to learn that even within the walls of a theological seminary sincere believers ask questions about

the meaning of faith. Recently, a retiring seminary president said, "In the last five years I have heard ten times
as many questions, and these were fifty times as hard as
students used to ask."

One seminary teacher, who has been severely criticised
for his book on Genesis, explains that he did not write
it to shake the faith of his students but to help them face
their real doubts and to give them some aid in working
through them. He said, "Only a man who has hardening of
the spiritual arteries has *no* doubts."

You can discover how Jesus dealt with the problem of
doubt in one of his disciples. The world still ridicules
Thomas as the doubter, but Jesus dealt with him gently.
You can learn a lesson from his experience.

I

A person must admit his doubt before anything can
be done about it. Thomas admitted his doubt. He was
honest about his skepticism. He was the only disciple not
present at the appearing on that first Easter night. He
had not seen the risen Christ, as the others had. He lacked
proof of the resurrection.

Thomas loved his Lord dearly. Consequently, he felt
defeated and dejected after the horror of the crucifixion. The situation so upset him that he could not bring
himself to meet with the disciples on that evening three
days later in an upper room.

When he heard the report of the excited disciples that
they had seen the risen Christ, he was skeptical. His doubt
was not as strong as disbelief. There is a difference in
the two. He did not say, "The resurrection is impossible."

He did say, "I will not believe until I have sufficient proof." He was more like an agnostic than an atheist.

A Christian should not feel guilty and anxious because he has doubt. Doubt is not a negation of faith but a definite part of faith. Paul Tillich calls attention to the element of insecurity in every truth, but a courageous faith asserts itself "in spite of" the recognized doubt. He describes it as a "confirmation of faith. It indicates the seriousness of the concern, its unconditional character."[1]

Harry Emerson Fosdick, who understands doubt from personal experience, reveals in one of his sermons the prevalence of this wrenching experience.

The trouble is that most Christians know about the faith of the great believers but not about their inner struggles. All Yale men here, and many more of us too, remember William Lyon Phelps. What a radiant Christian faith he had! But listen to him in his autobiography: "My religious faith remains in possession of the field only after prolonged civil war with my naturally sceptical mind." That experience belongs in the best tradition of the great believers. John Knox, the Scottish Reformer—what a man of conviction! Yes, but remember that time when his soul knew "anger, wrath and indignation, which it conceived against God, calling all his promises in doubt." Increase Mather—that doughty Puritan—what a man of faith! Yes, but read his diary and run on entries like this: "Greatly molested with temptations to atheism." Sing Luther's hymn, "A mighty fortress is our God," and one would suppose he never questioned his faith, but see him in other hours. "For more than a week," he wrote, "Christ was wholly lost. I was shaken by desperation and blasphemy against God."[2]

You need not be ashamed of honest doubt; possessing it places you in good company. A seeking doubt will not

harm your Christian faith. It would be better to have a
little pinch of honest doubt than a great heaping stack of
blind acceptance. The quality of doubt is often better than
the quantity of faith.

II

A person should seek a good environment for his doubt.
Thomas took his doubt somewhere. He did not sit brood-
ing on the housetop, but he met with the rest of the
disciples to learn of their testimonies and ideas. On the
following Sunday evening they held a clandestine meeting, perhaps in the same upper room of the Last Supper.
When the door had been well bolted, they began to ex-
claim about the recent appearances. All the disciples
were perplexed, but Thomas was completely baffled.

Thomas gives you a good example for dealing with
doubt. Get with the people who seem to have the answers. Discuss the problems with them. Seek for an
answer.

Fishing with a question mark is good religion. A little
questioning is as natural as the sucker that grows on the
tomato plant. But it has to be properly dealt with, or it
will become ruinous.

The person who is really in danger spiritually is the
one who has developed a skeptical approach to everything
but is too unconcerned to give much thought to the matter of faith. This attitude can lead to cynicism and despair.
The unconcerned skeptic continuously "stews in his own
juice." However, the person who has real questions and
doubts is concerned not just with himself but with truth.
He will seek answers on every side of the argument. If he

keeps working at his doubt, he will eventually come to custom-made beliefs of his own.

III

A doubting person should keep his mind open and should be ready for any contact with the truth. The doubt of Thomas came in contact with the proof he desired. Jesus returned to the disciples in order to manifest himself to Thomas. Every resurrection appearance of Jesus was made for a purpose. On this occasion the Master returned to deal with perplexed Thomas. Jesus did not condemn a doubter; rather he honored the doubt. Long before, he had dealt patiently with the messenger whom John the Baptist sent to ask, "Art thou he that should come, or do we look for another?" (Matt. 11:3).

Jesus appeared in order to convince Thomas of the reality of the resurrection. To the disciples he had proved himself real. They had thought him to be a spirit. On another occasion he ate fish to show them the reality of his return from the land from which no other traveler had returned.

Jesus presented the absolute and positive proof of his resurrection. He showed himself to be victor over death. He was a triumphant explorer returning from the cold arctic region of the tomb. Jesus gave the proof that would convince his disciples. He knew that Thomas was open-minded. Jesus knew that this proof would put an end to the incredulity of Thomas.

The best proof concerning religion is what a person experiences. An experiential religion is one that will hold its head high in the company of the haughty goddess of science. This kind of faith transcends doubt. A Christian worker recalled some words uttered by Ralph Sockman during the skeptical and roaring twenties: "Faith does not outrage reason; but it outruns it." Yes, faith cannot be proved by logic, but neither can logic disprove it. Doubts should vanish in the presence of overpowering proof.

If you do not accept proof after it is given, then you are as neutral as a swinging door. George Truett advised, "Do not be held down by the thralldom of captious doubts and speculative questions."

IV

Doubt can turn to faith. The doubt of Thomas turned to definite belief. After the proof was given, Thomas did not need to touch the crucifixion scars. Instead of reaching out his hand for further proof, he dropped to his knees, a convinced apostle. The proof satisfied him.

Jesus admonished him in this way: "Do not continue in unbelief, but in belief." The advice challenged Thomas. No longer did he vacillate between acceptance and rejection of the resurrection. He made a definite stand on the highway of truth, after he burned his bridges behind him.

Norman Vincent Peale reports how a paratrooper felt in the relation of facts to faith.

"The first time I jumped from a plane," a paratrooper told me, "everything in me resisted. All there was between death and me was a piece of cord and a little patch of silk, but when I actually found out for myself that the patch of silk would hold me, I had the most marvelous feeling of exultation in all my life. I wasn't afraid of anything and the release from fear filled me with exquisite delight. I really did not want to come down; I was actually happy."[3]

Thomas expressed his faith in these simple yet eloquent words: "My Lord and my God." With that statement the doubting apostle turned his question mark into an exclamation point.

V

A person who works out a confident faith will be richly rewarded. The transformed doubt of Thomas was blessed by Jesus. Even though our Lord had honored genuine doubt, he blessed a confirmed faith.

Jesus had a word for others of his day and ours. He put a greater blessing on those who would arrive at the truth of his divinity with a lesser amount of proof. "Thomas, because thou hast seen me, thou hast believed: blessed are they that have not seen, and yet have believed" (John 20:29).

Today Jesus provides the necessary amount of proof for us to *know* the essentials of his religion. We can be sure of his divinity, of the efficacy of prayer, and other such doctrines.

Consequently, if you have some doubts, do not feel guilty but deal with those doubts as Thomas did. Admit them, and then take them into a good environment. Listen to the proof on the subject. Then make a definite commitment, one way or the other. Often, a mature religion is hammered out in the workshop of doubt. Jesus will bless your endeavor, and you will have the joy of turning your question marks into exclamation points for him.

4

Living in an Age of Anxiety

THIS SHOULD be an era of security. Gone are the economic woes of the thirties, the sexual repression of the Victorian age, the morbid religion of horse and buggy days, the tyranny of management over labor, and the vulnerable disarmament of the twenties. But no paradise of confidence has resulted.

Money in the bank, a second car in the carport, a boat, and a summer house do not produce a feeling of security. Many people who have acquired these luxuries compulsively take tranquilizers.

Some teen-agers, with no strong code of taboos, engage in premarital sexual relations. They discover that this new freedom does not set them free. They worry about communicating fully and successfully in the sex act. They wonder why they have guilt feelings, and they become anxious.

Many educated people have discarded ideas of heaven and hell. Consequently, they have no hope to work for and no fear of punishment to deter them from mistakes.

Without guidance, their freedom turns into anxiety.

Labor unions are insisting on cutting hours from the work week, when now the average laborer worries over what to do with all his leisure time.

Technology is producing megatons of destructive protection. President Lyndon Johnson recently revealed that the United States and Russia separately have stockpiled enough nuclear explosives to average ten tons of TNT for every man, woman, and child on earth. Who can feel secure sitting on just one ton of TNT?

Progress has not produced security; it has contributed to making this an age of anxiety. Yet you cannot say, "Stop the world, and let me off." You must look beyond the science and technology of this century for an answer. Modern medicine does not have a miracle drug for the sickness of this age.

We are like the disciples in a storm. Even though some of them were experienced fishermen, one of the land lubbers in the crew began to grow agitated when the wind whistled and the waves sloshed. Contagious fear spread to the others. If their boat had been equipped with a panic button, they would have pushed it. They believed that their last hour had arrived. In their agitated pessimism, they scolded Jesus for sleeping during the emergency. Too often, we are willing to surrender to unknown terrors, and we blame the Master for his lack of sympathy.

Perhaps your main worry is not as specific as a storm. If you find it difficult to explain, perhaps you have anxiety instead of fear. If someone were to aim a pistol at your head, you would have a legitimate fear. However, if you became lost in a forest and began to worry about starving, being shot at, or being attacked by a wild animal, then you would be developing a good case of anxiety. Fear is a reaction to specific danger. Anxiety is the feeling of diffuseness, uncertainty, and helplessness in the face of an undefined threat. Fear is rational; anxiety is irrational.

When a dog becomes alarmed, it hesitates and cocks its ears and breathes carefully. It seems to be asking, "What happens next?" This preparatory questioning is a sentinel function; it readies him to meet whatever may develop. Human beings have a similar reaction. The state of anxiety seems to be this phase of constant expectation and dread of the unknown.

Surely, the Great Physician does not want the world to continue suffering from this disease. He can assist us in fighting this space-age illness by helping us to recognize its symptoms.

I

One of the symptoms is the threat of defeat. This threat becomes a real problem when it is perceived from the moral angle. In other words, many anxious people are afraid of meeting temptation unsuccessfully. Do you know what your own temptations are? If you do not know what your main temptations are, you are in deadly peril; for they can slip up on you and throw an enslaving net about you. However, if you know what they are, you can be on your guard.

An athletic young man was strongly attracted to an older woman. He wondered if it would not be permissible to have an affair with her. He reasoned that the harm

had already been done, since the Sermon on the Mount
calls lust in the heart "adultery." When he wrote a mature
Christian for his views, he received the following answer:

Of course it is not as bad to think evil as it is to do it. Jesus
nowhere says that the act is just as bad as the thought. What
Jesus was trying to help us to see was that the lustful thought
precedes the lustful act. Every person is tempted. The proof
that he is on God's side is that he resists temptation. Other-
wise, we become bellhops to our own passions. The Epistle to
the Hebrews says that Jesus "was in all points tempted like
as we are, yet without sin" (Heb. 4:15). If Christ was tempted,
we should not expect to avoid it ourselves.[1]

Many people today are living defeated lives. They are
finding no way to meet temptations victoriously. They
are living in a constant dread of some overwhelming
power.

Perhaps you are anxious over the fact that you have
no assurance you can prevail over temptation; thus you
live in the shadow of defeat—like an inferior football team
that knows it will lose. Similarly, you are fighting half-
heartedly.

Sometimes this defeatist and pessimistic attitude spills
over into the rest of life. A person loses all confidence
that he will succeed in his life goals. He knows that his
efforts will be unsuccessful, and he puts forth only a token
attempt. A defeated attitude is one of the symptoms
of this age of anxiety.

When we look at the present status of man, we are
tempted to agree with these pessimistic words of T. S.
Eliot:

Where is the wisdom we have lost in knowledge?
Where is the knowledge we have lost in information?
The cycles of Heaven in twenty centuries
Bring us farther from God and nearer to the Dust.[2]

Our religion, however, has a cure for this symptom.
A positive and confident faith can dry up the mildew
of defeat. Jesus gives confidence to one who wants to
overcome temptation. Our Lord, who was tempted in all
points like as we and yet without sin, promises strength
for our weakness. After he muzzled the storm, Jesus asked
his anxious companions why they were so frightened:
"What has happened to your faith?" (Luke 8:25, Phillips).

We need to make the great discovery of Christ's power,
and then we can face life confidently. The Greek mathe-
matician Archimedes discovered the principle of the
lever. He took a fulcrum and an iron bar and showed the
king how to move a great weight with very little force.
Then confidently he said to his king, "Give me somewhere
to stand, and I will move the world." You will swell with
that same confidence when you find the leverage of
trusting faith.

The disciples had thought they were drowning. They
were trying to diagnose the case for the Great Physician.
They saw only defeat and failure. But Jesus corrected
their wrong thoughts. He gave them peace. Just as Jesus
quieted the storm on the lake, he will also still the storms
of temptation. He can release within you the same
power that caused the men in that little boat to be filled
with awe instead of anxiety.

Just because the world is changing so rapidly does not
mean that you should have less hope. Your ideas may

change, but you can still hang on to the confidence of Jesus' power within your life. An illustration of this idea in the educational world occurred when Bertrand Russell celebrated his eightieth birthday. He stated that there were some things he felt he would never learn; in fact, there were things he hoped he would never learn. "I don't wish to learn to change my hopes for the world," he said. "I am prepared to change my beliefs about the state of the world, but not my hopes." Then he described his life as eighty years of changing beliefs but unchanging hopes. It is not surprising that such an idealist would send telegrams of mediation to Premier Khrushchev and President Kennedy in the East-West power struggle. You need that same spirit of confident optimism in order to face anxiety over defeat.

II

Another evidence of anxiety is the highly competitive nature of our society. You learn from your culture that you must push to achieve and shove to succeed. You learn to win by forcing others to fail. Thus this joy in another's failure is a cruel expression of insecurity.

Children today learn this cruel competition from rivalry with brothers and sisters and from the school system. From the first day of kindergarten to the last degree of graduate school, surpassing others is the main task. In one of the finest books on this subject, *The Meaning of Anxiety*, Rollo May makes the statement that *"individual competitive success is both the dominant goal in our culture and the most pervasive occasion for anxiety."*[3]

The only remedy for this condition is an attitude that

can lift the person out of the walls of his own life. He needs to look beyond these walls and feel himself to be a part of the world. Alfred Adler, the psychologist, offers a solution. Anxiety, he says, "can be dissolved solely by that bond which binds the individual to humanity. Only that individual can go through life without anxiety who is conscious of belonging to the fellowship of man."[4]

There is a need for an organized fellowship of mankind. People need to be a part of it. They need to lose themselves in this cause which is greater than themselves. The fellowship of Christian love within the church is the best antidote for the poison of competition.

III

Another symptom of this age's anxiety is the hostility that is latent in almost every person. It takes very little annoyance from one of your neighbors or one of the men in your business to make you feel like cursing him. Really, the anger and the hostility are already there; the neighbor merely gives you an opportunity to release them.

Often the real hostility results from the fact that you harbor resentment against someone on whom you are dependent. The small child is dependent on the strong parent; he thinks twice before he expresses resentment or disgust. The child knows that he receives material and emotional security from the father or mother, and he does not want to endanger this supply of security. Similarly, in later life any overly dependent person will always have some deep resentments against the person he depends on, whether husband, wife, or child. Now this repressed hatred will boil and bubble within the kettle of the soul until it burns itself out or explodes. And every bubble causes more anxiety and unhappiness in the life of the person.

So Paul advises: do not let the sun go down on your wrath. Express it. Do anything with it, but do not go to bed angry.

One hot Saturday afternoon in Georgia I was pushing a coughing lawn mower, and my wife called to me, "You can't come to the phone, can you?"

"Of course I can," I replied, grateful for the interruption. On the line was a young deacon of the church I had previously served. I wondered what he could possibly want with me. When he asked to come to talk with me that afternoon, I urged him to come ahead.

When the serious young man arrived, he went straight to the point. "While you were my pastor, I did not give you the support you should have had. When people criticized your program, I didn't say a thing. I committed the sin of silence, and I have felt bad about it ever since."

There were hostilities and resentments there he had never expressed, but mutely he had stored them up. Now he believed that his Christian influence and his personal happiness were at stake, unless he got this hostile anxiety off his chest. He apologized for his negative attitudes and requested that we both pray. One of the memorable moments of my ministry occurred when I heard this man have courage enough to say, "I'm sorry. I want you to pray for me and pray with me." He rose from his knees with a lighter emotional load. Then less troubled in mind, he returned to work in his church.

Defeat, competition, and hostility are three of the symptoms of this age of anxiety. They are hazards, but they are not unconquerable foes. When they appear in our lives, we can let Christ say to them, "Peace, be still."

A Prayer for Overcoming Anxiety

O Christ, we need thy calming presence in our troubled lives; at a time when we are agitated and disturbed, we know thou art near and can speak words of peace. At this moment, may we realize thy command over the universe, and may we lose our fear on the smooth surface of the sea of thy love.

O Jesus, thou who wast victorious over every temptation, give us that same sure victory. Give us meaning in our lives.

We feel ourselves changing in thy serene presence. Even now thou art taking away the defeat, the hostility, and the bitterness in our lives. We praise thee for thy marvelous works. Amen.

5

Is Worry a Sin?

WORRY IS never insignificant. Many of the worries that people have are over little things, but insignificant matters can grow irritatingly important. Chester Swor tells of his first year as a teacher at Mississippi College, when he was given the responsibility of supervising Crestman Hall dormitory. Everything got on his nerves, and he worried about the most trivial matters. He got upset when the boys put butter on the doorknobs and when they rolled garbage cans down the hall. These things were neither collegiate nor in good taste, but he decided to write them on a list and to mark them off. He said he would save his worries for more important things. This technique made his life a lot smoother and gave him more energy for important matters.

Once a whaling vessel stopped at a South Sea island for water and provisions. While many of the crew were off on the island, cannibals came and took possession of the ship and bound the men who were left guarding it. The crew, on returning, saw the situation and scattered a keg of tacks on the deck of the vessel. These stuck in the bare feet of the savages and sent them howling into the sea. They had been ready to meet sword and spear, but they could not overcome the tacks on the floor. Little worries can be like these tacks. Although they seem insignificant, they can bring about defeat. Little worries can conquer people who are alert only to the danger of big calamities.

I

Worry is not as hard to handle as anxiety. There is a difference in anxiety and worry. Anxiety is vague; worry is definite. Anxiety is unsure; worry is pessimistic. Anxiety is more subconscious; worry is more conscious. Thus, worry is easier to deal with than anxiety.

Once a person grew disgusted with a steady diet of worry. He stopped to analyze his fretful habits, and he made the following statistical discoveries:

40 per cent of his worries would never happen.
30 per cent of his worries were about old decisions which could not be altered.
12 per cent of his worries were about others' criticisms of himself, mostly untrue and made by people who felt inferior.
10 per cent of his worries were about his health, which would get worse from the worry.
8 per cent of his worries were legitimate, since life has some real problems to meet.[1]

There is a difference in worry and concern. No one can keep from being concerned when he is overdrawn at the bank or when a member of his family is ill. He will show concern when a child gets into trouble or when his wife is killed in an automobile wreck, but he will not completely lose his trust in God's protective love.

Worry is concern taken to an extreme. Concern shows interest, but worry shows despair. Worry runs a treadmill, getting nowhere. Concern moves toward the destination of helpful action. Worry crosses bridges beforehand; concern takes along a boat, to be used if needed. Worry expels religion, but concern brings one's cares to the Good Shepherd.

An old farmer said, "If you can do something about a problem, then you should be concerned. But if you can't do anything, then worry is just like running a mill when there is no grist to grind. All that it does is to wear out the mill."

I know a woman who worried about her husband while he was overseas in the war. When the fighting was over and he was returning home, he was run over by a taxi and killed. Then she realized how useless her worries had been.

II

Worry is wrong under certain circumstances. Jesus pointed out that anxiety over food, drink, and dress are unnecessary. Life is greater than what sustains it, and there is no need to worry about it. Worry ignores God's fatherly concern. Peter Marshall suggested that we are like a child bringing a broken toy for a father to fix. When the father agrees to repair the toy, the child, instead of standing back and waiting, moves in close to offer a lot of needless advice. Then he gets impatient and gets his little hands in the father's way. If we had more trust when we pray, we could wait for God to work things out. Sometimes we try to interpose our own will and try to make circumstances come about as we would wish them.

Someone has made the following comparisons of worry and prayer:

Prayer is my acknowledgment of faith;
Worry is my denial of faith.
Prayer is putting my hand into God's, trusting to His loving guidance;
Worry is withdrawing my hand, and denying His power to lead me.
Prayer leads through the door of faith into the presence of God;
Worry leads through the door of anxiety into the darkness of loneliness and discouragement.
If prayer does not cancel worry,
Worry will cancel prayer.

Worry detracts from a person's Christian influence. A child once said to a missionary, "Do you really believe that God is your heavenly father?"

He answered, "Of course, I do."

The child said, "If God is like a father and cares for us, why do you worry so much?" This child had a discerning question. You cannot have worry and deep trust at the same time.

III

The effect of worry is damaging. The Orientals long ago invented a type of torture in which a person is strapped down and a small amount of water is allowed to drip continually on his skull. It would take a long time for this dropping of water to do any physical damage, but it does not take long for it to take an emotional toll and to do mental damage. Worry has led many people to ulcers, migraine headaches, and other illnesses.

"Worry will kill you," said the conscientious mother of a teen-age boy. She was upset over discovering that he had been smoking without her permission. He was seeking, in reality, to prove by this habit and by asserting his independence in other ways that he was grown.

When I first talked with the mother, she spoke of a catching pain in her side. Later she said that worry had made her ill. "It makes you sick. It makes God seem unreal, and it makes other people seem unimportant."

Of course, worry is harmful. But you wonder if it is a sin. I believe that the extent of worry determines whether or not it is a sin. It is difficult to say at what point it becomes demonic and ungodly. I do not know at what level chronic worry displaces God, but I do not want to take a chance on reaching that point. I would like to rid my life of every trace of it, wouldn't you?

IV

There is a way out of worry. According to William James' book, *The Varieties of Religious Experience*, Horace Fletcher once said to himself, "If it is possible to get rid of anger and worry, why is it necessary to have them at all?"[2] Once he asked himself this question, then he saw a new horizon opening up in his life without worry. He proved it to himself shortly afterwards when he missed a train because of a bellboy's tardiness in getting his baggage from the hotel room to the train station.

When Mr. Fletcher saw the train pull out he was naturally disappointed, but he did not scold the bellboy. He said to him, "It doesn't matter at all, you couldn't help it, so we will try again tomorrow. Here is your fee, I am sorry you had all this trouble in earning it."[3] The bellboy returned the next day and refused to accept another cent for his service. He had been amply paid by a man who refused to worry about a small incident.

A person who loses his worries can relax and sleep. One of my favorite Scripture verses is found in Psalm 127:2, "He giveth his beloved sleep." Jesus proved the truth of this verse. He slept through a storm. He was not worried and agitated about the boat sinking or about the impression someone else might have. He simply slept, because he trusted in God's goodness. He exemplified with his life the teaching that one should take no thought for tomorrow.

Another person who lived this same teaching was Paul. He wrote from his first Roman imprisonment (although he did not know it was his first imprisonment; he thought it was his last), "Be careful for nothing" (Phil. 4:6). The New English Bible translates this verse, "Have no anxiety." The apostle Paul in prison was not worried and disturbed.

Dale Carnegie writes about another person who had this same kind of serenity. He went to interview Henry Ford a few years prior to Mr. Ford's death. Before he met him, he expected to see strains of the long years that Ford had spent in building up and managing one of the world's greatest businesses. Mr. Carnegie was surprised to see how calm, well, and peaceful he looked at seventy-eight. When he asked him if he ever worried, Mr. Ford replied, "No, I believe God is managing the affairs and that he doesn't need any advice from me. With God in charge, I believe that everything will work out for the best in the end. So what is there to worry about?"[4]

A Christian once grew concerned about the many broad and vague worries that spoil our lives. He worked out the following rules for worrying scientifically:

1. Never worry over rumors or what "they" say. First get the facts.
2. Know definitely your worry problem. Write it down. Face it.
3. Worry about only one problem at a time.
4. Never worry in bed, in the dining room, or at church.
5. Set a time limit. If you must go beyond it, give yourself credit for time and a half.
6. Never worry alone. Take it to the Lord.

It had been a dry summer, and a farmer told me that his crops were ruined. He was worried. Then he told of his sister, an invalid in a nursing home, who had begun to insist that he bring her home. This bachelor farmer was worried about how he could take care of her. Then he told of dropping a heavy trailer tongue on his toe. He was worried about how long it would take to heal.

The next Sunday he attended church. But during the afternoon he visited the nursing home and became despondent over the helplessness of his sister. That night he drove his car behind a cotton gin and shot himself.

Among his personal effects was found this note: "Many reasons. Sick, nervous, worried, depressed." One could almost say that he "worried himself to death."

Do not let worry defeat your life. Get rid of it. Follow this wonderful advice from the Scriptures: "Casting all your care upon him, for he careth for you" (1 Peter 5:7).

6

Love Breaks the Apron Strings

EVERY HOSPITAL provides protection for the premature baby. In a plexiglass incubator the atmosphere is kept at a constant temperature and humidity. This isolated crib is vitally important for a fragile new baby, but it would be a prison for a healthy toddler.

The family provides an incubator for childhood religion. In this protected environment a fragile young faith develops and grows. Most young people outgrow the need for this protection, and they leave behind its precautions as they boldly emerge into a world of scientific question and materialistic idolatry.

Sometimes conscientious parents will try to force the youthful personality back into the incubator. They reason that he is not ready for the extreme temperatures of the world or for the knocks it will inflict. But the young person knows his own capacities. He feels imprisoned by protection. The only exit for this young person is to break out.

Parents and children alike need to recognize the val-

58 CONQUERING INNER SPACE

uable protection of family life, but they also need to become aware of its limitations. You can discover a balanced view in Jesus' life. He was deeply devoted to his family; yet he found a superior claim. He heard a call transcending all family demands.

I

Jesus teaches that respect is necessary. By his example and his teaching, he affirms the importance of the family.

This generation needs Jesus' view of respect and reverence for the family. Modern children consider such respect as out of date as the horse-drawn carriage, the mustache cup, and the stereoscope. In many homes tempers flare at the turn of a channel, and youngsters learn from TV that daddies are clumsy clods and mommies are soured sirens. With some families, love is a many-splintered thing. Their epitaph might read: They lived scrappily ever after.

The respect Jesus teaches is a sincere expression of kindness. This devotion is not blind to all faults, but it is magnanimous enough to look beyond them to virtues. It is based on an appreciation of persons for their own sakes.

The loveliest picture of his devotion occurs in the most unlikely place. Under the storm clouds of Golgotha when life is ebbing, Jesus is sensitive to every pain but is not emotionally conquered by the negative feeling on that hill. He does not curse his betrayer, cry for vengeance on his executioners, nor blame his followers for their timidity. In that hour, pregnant with possibilities, he shows concern for his mother.

From the cross he says, "Woman, behold thy son!" (John 19:26). He knows that Mary will need help. He guesses that she will be unable to meet financial responsibilities. He imagines that in her old age she will become childish and forgetful, needing someone to watch after her. He knows that with the apostle of love to watch after her soul's needs, she will not sink into the ocean of despair and revenge. Jesus is thinking of these needs when he says to John, "Behold thy mother!" (19:27).

You can have that same quality of love. Perhaps God has given you an aged person to live in the home with you. If so, accept this responsibility and its limitations of freedom with a feeling of joyful duty.

A woman once said to me, "All I can see that my daughter learned from an expensive college education was to drink and to be rude to her parents." We should lose such adolescent attitudes of rebellion and resentment. We should mature with a love like that of Jesus, that responds with good will, regardless of whether or not it is deserved.

II

Jesus finds that a break with his family is necessary. Consequently, there is a deep conflict that develops in his life. He recognizes that his family has been the most meaningful and influential source in his early life. However, the family hinders him in his work. Just as Jesus is getting started, when he most needs the encouragement and co-operation of his family, he receives discouragement and interference. We can see these developments in three illustrations from his early life and ministry.

Notice the boy in the Temple. Here is a lad who is suntanned and bronzed from healthy play out of doors. Yet he is coming into a questioning period of life, when the answers he seeks will be found in the human heart and not in the beauties of nature. You understand something of the coming conflict when you see him completely forget about the group he is traveling with. He disregards any instructions about meeting his family at a certain place and a certain time. Something more important has intervened.

The confident parents have traveled a day's distance from the city, when they begin to look for him among the kinsfolk and friends. For a brief but frantic period of time they search for him in Jerusalem. When they discover him in the Temple, they are both relieved and vexed at his disregard. "Why have you done us this way? We have been frantic with worry."

The boy's reply comes like a clap of thunder on a hot, sunny day. He says (literally translated), "Know ye not that I must be in the things of my father?" (Luke 2:49).

The brusk reply confuses the devoted parents. He is speaking with adolescent knowledge, the kind that is beginning to grasp facts but lacks the framework of experience to stack these facts upon. His words are like the first streaks of light in the morning sky, foretelling a dawn that will quickly follow.

This is a strange episode. The rough edges of this story are smoothed off for us by the comment that the boy returns home with his puzzled parents and is again "subject unto them."

As he grows older these same conflicts recur. See him

at the festivities of the wedding at Cana. In the middle of the celebration a feverish and excited woman pushes through the crowd to Jesus. "They have no wine," his mother announces to him in distress.

Strange to our ears are the words the Master says to his mother, "Woman, what have I to do with thee?" (John 2:4). We can only guess at their meaning. It is possible he was rejecting her impatience and her orders. Perhaps his mother was expecting no miracle, but she wanted Jesus and his friends to go out and procure supplies in order that the people would praise her. Nevertheless, he rejects her suggestion in a kind tone of voice.

He performs a sign at that time to demonstrate a lesson to the people at the feast. He symbolically shows them that the religion he is bringing to them far surpasses anything they have previously experienced.

Next, recall a scene where Jesus is teaching. He tells his eager hearers that for one to be a disciple he must *hate* his father, mother, wife, and children (Luke 14:26). You are shocked by the word he chooses. "Hate" is a vivid word. But remember that he is not an American speaking. He has not oversentimentalized family relationships, as many of us have.

The Master is speaking in terms of greater and lesser loyalties. Love for God should be so different from love of family, that in comparison it would appear to be hatred.

With such teachings, however, people began to wonder about his sanity. They treated him like you and I would. They said, "He is beside himself." We do not dare to form such words on our lips. Nevertheless, from the way we treat his teachings, we, too, demonstrate that we think he is a dreaming idealist—impractical and unsound. I can see him coming into one of our banks for a loan and being turned down. "Too unstable and no sense of responsibility," we declare. In effect, when we turn him down for this loan, we are saying with his family, "He is mad." What we need today is an overwhelming sense of his sanity.

When Jesus found that a break was absolutely necessary, he deftly and lovingly cut restraining family ties. This severing of hindering ties is the most difficult part of today's adjustment to family relationships. The only affection some children know is smother love. They are dominated by the woman of the house. She wears the pants in the family, but she covers them with a beguiling apron; and the apron strings are made of steel. For a few people, there must be a cutting of these apron strings before there can be any freedom of the soul. Only the most thoughtful Christian can perform this procedure without hurting others and without being hurt.

Every step on life's road brings the Christian farther from his birth and family. But he should not use the words of Jesus as an excuse to be rude and unloving. Constantly he should ask, "Is this attitude wilful pride, or is it a step toward mature independence?" When he gets these matters in perspective, he can move ahead with confidence and enthusiasm.

III

Jesus teaches respect for the family. He demonstrates that a break is sometimes necessary. But then he teaches that we should go beyond both by recognizing the true, larger family. Jesus introduces us to the real family.

Again, see Jesus teaching an eager group. People are crowding close, fascinated by this simple teacher who looks like one of them but talks like a prophet from God. Then a messenger elbows his way through the crowd. He says that the mother and brothers of the new rabbi are outside wanting him to come with them. Strange timing! This request occurs just after his friends have called him mad. Perhaps the family partially agrees and sends a person to call him back to the privacy of family living. When the messenger cannot get to the speaker, he yells this information aloud. There is a dramatic pause, and the crowd waits to see what will happen. Then Jesus says, "Who is my mother, or my brethren? . . . whosoever shall do the will of God" (Mark 3:33-35).

You have learned what it means to be a part of this larger family. You have felt the close ties; you have felt the sustaining hand about your shoulder. You have felt a relation that others have not understood. Which one of us has not received words of wisdom from some old church member others call a "fogy"?

It is normal that we move from the family into the wider bond of the Christian fellowship. A theologian has said that the Christian church "creates a community which is as intimate and as strong as the family relation, and at the same time infinitely superior to it."

Even Sigmund Freud, who usually was extremely critical, on one occasion praised religion as "a safe mooring; it lowered the importance of his family relationships, and thus protected him from the threat of isolation by giving him access to the great community of mankind."[1]

A person who feels called into Christ's service will put the claims of his family in a subordinate place. Just as the soldier cannot refuse the call to his country's need because he has a young wife with an infant at her breast, neither can the Christian soldier dodge the divine draft because of family responsibilities.

Florence Nightingale felt a divine call to leave home. Her family strongly objected to her plans to go to a distant battlefield for the purpose of nursing the wounded. Her mother said, "We are ducks who have hatched a wild swan."[2]

Another who had to disregard his family in order to follow God was John Bunyan. He was told to choose between ceasing to preach or going to prison. He stated his dilemma in these words:

The parting with my Wife and poor Children hath often been to me in this place as the pulling the Flesh from my Bones; and that not only because I am somewhat too fond of these great Mercies, but also because I should have often brought to mind the many hardships, miseries and wants that my poor Family was like to meet with, should I be taken from them, *especially my poor blind Child*, who lay nearer my heart than all I had besides . . . I was as a man who was pulling down his House upon the Head of his Wife and Children; *yet*, thought I, *I must do it, I must do it*.[3]

Such choices are still being made by brave Christians. I know a man who has recently flown to the mission field, despite the objections of his parents. The older people, without the same sense of devotion, could scarcely understand his previous call to the ministry, much less his subsequent call to the foreign mission field. With patience and love, he tried to explain his decision. But he did not base his going on whether or not they would approve. He said, "Jesus has called, and I must follow."

Such decisions for Christ expand one's relationships to Christ's larger family. I know a college senior who had never joined a church because one parent had been Catholic and the other Protestant. Consequently, she had put off any decision. As younger students began to come to her for advice, she began to realize some of the things she lacked, despite the fact that she was a campus leader. "They could take their problems to a much better counselor than I. They could go to God."

One day, in the middle of a conversation, a faculty friend asked about her church membership. This dedicated teacher invited the student to drop by her apartment whenever she felt a need to talk. The senior reported the outcome to me in these words:

Perhaps a week later in a moment of depression, I went to her. We talked, or rather she talked to me about Christ, the church, and the reasons that I had rejected these. She did not prod me or try to make me feel uncomfortable. She answered many questions, but more important stimulated my interest so that I wanted to seek the answers myself. She suggested several books and Scriptures that might be of help. Before leaving she led us in prayer, asking God to guide me in my search for him. This touched me deeply. I went to sleep that night feeling as I had never felt before. . . . Through this experience I found God. I also learned to appreciate the meaning of Christian fellowship and Christian friendship.

Each person must work out his own answers to the

problem of family ties. For a few, it will necessitate an abrupt break with dominating parents. Anyone who must leave his family for Christ will find a new family relationship that surpasses anything he has ever known.

However, for you it might likely mean maintaining a balance of mature independence and respectful devotion within your family. Do you express appreciation to your family? Perhaps you need to unbutton your lips and release some words of gratitude and concern. You can learn to forget childish grudges and live in the present. You can keep the lines of family communication open. You can look forward to the day when you, as a parent, will be willing to release your child to the world's inhospitable climate.

You can also learn a new appreciation of the church as God's family. You can promote good will and a deepened fellowship within its circle. The church as a family can provide a source of strength necessary for the growing soul.

7

Saints in Overalls

IF YOU want to make a youngster angry, just call him a "saint." He will hate the word. A boy in trouble, trying to excuse his misdeed, said, "Well, I ain't no saint, you know. I never claimed to be. Who wants to be a saint, anyway?"

Adults react to the word in a similar way. There are some people who had rather be called a "liar" than a "saint." Somehow they have gotten the idea that a saint is a "goody-goody," a "Holy Joe."

The word "saint" is used throughout the Bible without any such odor attached to it. It was a good word when it was included in the Scriptures, and we need to understand it in the original sense in order to comprehend the Bible. We need to see what saints are like in order to develop our own lives.

I

In the first place, saints are people who have met the Master. Since when are saints dead people? We have come to think of them as unusually holy people who have died and gone on to receive their reward. But study your New Testament; you will find that, in about every case, the word "saint" is used to refer to a living Christian.

Paul addressed six of his letters to people who are called saints. Certainly, he was not writing a letter to heaven; he was writing to struggling people who were trying to follow the path of the Master. Typical is the verse that opens the epistle to the Philippians. "Paul and Timotheus, the servants of Jesus Christ, to all the saints in Christ Jesus which are at Philippi, with the bishops and deacons" (Phil. 1:1). A similar verse opens the first letter to the Corinthians, those people who had greatly disappointed him as Christians, and yet he designated them "sanctified," called to be saints. We need to get out of our minds the idea that saints are perfect people or that they are dead people.

One of the modern translators of the Bible, J. B. Phillips, has omitted in several places the traditional word because of misunderstanding. In the address of the letter to the Romans, where they are "called to be saints," he substitutes "called to be Christ's men and women."

Saints were living people who had met the Master but still had earthly needs. They were usually not rich people. The book of Acts refers to the ministering to the needs of the saints and taking an offering for the saints. They were common, ordinary men and women whom the Master called, and whom he commissioned to carry on his work. The writer of Jude refers to the faith which was "once delivered unto the saints."

When you understand sainthood in this way, you see

that it is no disgrace to be called a saint in the twentieth century; it is an honor. A saint does not refer to a person who has merely joined a church; it means a person who has actually confronted Christ, alone, depending upon no merit of his own, simply trusting in the mercy of the Lord. A saint is one who has found his way in life and is now oriented on a pilgrimage toward the Holy City. A saint is one who has found the answer to the question, "What can wash away my sin?" A saint is one who has found an answer to the problem of meaninglessness in this age. A saint is one who continues to find moral strength in a world that is drunk with pleasure and gone crazy over sensuality.

II

In the second place, saints are people who are radiant. A little girl who had always attended an old stone church with beautiful stained-glass windows was asked the definition of saints. "They are people the light shines through." She was correct. Saints are radiant people.

A saint uses ordinary tools and makes something special. I can never forget the time that I saw some ordinary-looking tools on a table. They were similar to a carpenter's saw, chisel, hammer, and brace and bit. But they were a surgeon's. He was operating on a sailor who had been in the South Pacific during a typhoon when his head hit against the bulkhead of a ship. He had been flown to San Diego for this delicate operation. The surgeon using these tools removed a large portion of his skull and inserted a silver plate. It was a marvelous operation.

The ordinary Christian is like that. He uses ordinary

tools to do something extraordinary in the spiritual realm. The saint takes a gloomy Monday and makes something special of it. A janitor sweeps in corners where an inspector would never look, because he is dedicated in his work. A lighthouse keeper rows out night after night to the lonely rock, though he knows that for weeks no ship goes by his coast. He does it because he is counted on for that. A shut-in, rather than bogging down in self-pity, spends time in sending others "get well" cards.

One of the greatest needs today is a rediscovery of calling in a vocation. Perhaps God wants to use you right where you are. He needs saints in overalls, people who will still be Christian despite bickering workers around them, a grumpy foreman over them, or a tired soul within them. He needs people who will "pray devoutly and hammer stoutly."

God calls busy people. Some people do not think that a pastor has enough to keep him busy. A minister out fishing one Monday morning was scolded by a deacon, "Remember, Preacher, the devil don't take no holiday."

"No," the reply came. "But I haven't taken him for my model." After this break in routine, the minister returned to his work.

God uses busy people. He called Moses from tending the flock. Gideon was threshing wheat. Saul was searching for the livestock. Elisha was busy plowing with twelve teams of oxen. Peter, Andrew, James, and John were busy with their fishing nets when the Master called them. Lydia was busy dyeing fabrics purple, in order to make a living, when she was called to service. God uses busy, radiant saints.

Most people who apply for a job today are concerned about what they will get. "How much time off will I get? How much security do I have? What are my retirement benefits?" These are their questions. Seldom do they inquire about the actual work they will be paid to do. It is no wonder that people call this the "age of the goof-off," the "age of the coffee break," and the "age of the inferior product."

Typical is the ambition of Linus in the comic strip:

When I get big, I'm going to be a humble little country doctor. I'll live in the city, see, and every morning I'll get up, climb into my sports car and zoom into the country! Then I'll start healing people . . . I'll heal everybody for miles around! I'll be a world famous humble little country doctor![1]

Such mixed-up thinking is not limited to the funny papers. Many others are just as confused in their goals.

We need to return to the principle of hard, honest work as the fulfilment of destiny. A person can discover his purpose in God's world through work.

Before the time of Benedict, monks spent most of their hours roaming the streets, begging. He brought them together in monasteries that became largely self-supporting. Most of their day was spent in work—hard, manual labor. In the time that was left, they studied and meditated. They chose this striking motto: *Laborare est orare*—"To work is to pray."

President Ellis Fuller of Southern Baptist Theological Seminary, shortly before his death, was inspecting the construction of the new chapel he had dreamed about and prayed about. He was conscious of the money being paid the construction crew, and he crawled up a ladder to ask a workman why he was taking so long on one corner.

The man replied, "My father and grandfather were both plasterers, and we consider it an art. I want to do a thorough job on this corner. If ever in worship anyone looks up to this corner, he will not be distracted by poor work."

A great need in this age of mediocrity is for people to take their work more seriously. A Christian's vocation can be an opportunity for radiance as a twentieth-century saint.

III

Saints are people who are heroic in the face of danger. The following words of consolation from the psalmist must have been written to people who were in difficult trouble: "For the Lord loveth judgment, and forsaketh not his saints; they are preserved for ever" (Psalm 37:28).

When the situation is perilous, the true worth of a person will show up. Those with no inner core of stability will begin to tremble with terror. The saint, armed with his faith, becomes as confident as a soldier with a new rifle.

One such modern saint was Dietrich Bonhoeffer, a young German pastor of brilliant mind and deep commitment. He happened to be in America when war broke out in 1939. He was urged by American friends to stay away from Germany and use his scholarly and pastoral gifts in this country. But his primary view was that Christian obedience compelled him to assume responsibility in the place where circumstances required him. Thus, he returned to Germany and threw himself into the resistance against Nazism. He was arrested in April, 1943, and after two years in prison was executed by special order of Heinrich Himmler. The title of one of his books reflects the deep conviction of his heroic life, *The Cost of Discipleship*.

Another modern saint, heroic in the face of danger, was Dr. William Wallace. Many people left China while there was opportunity to escape. He remained during the Japanese invasion of the thirties, during World War II, and during the Communist take-over. He practiced medicine at every opportunity, even performing surgery during an air raid. Without any sanctimonious display, he lived a devoted Christian life. He died in a Communist prison, patient and heroic to the end.

Like Bonhoeffer and Wallace, you are a saint. All believers are saints. With such splendid titles, we all should live splendid lives.

8

Sometimes Up—
Sometimes Down

CLARENCE TOOK his religion so seriously that he even suggested abolishing youth group parties at the church and sending the money to foreign missions. He grew so morbid and introspective about his faith that no one wanted to be around him.

Frances seemed frivolous. She was always so happy and giddy about her religion that she seemed shallow. Even at serious times, she wore such a broad smile and said so much about joy and peace of mind that she seemed slightly out of touch with reality.

Sybil felt tendencies to alternate in the directions of sadness and of elation at various times. She concluded that religion caused these mood swings, and she decided to give up Christianity.

Perhaps you have had a similar experience. With an immature faith, you have drifted about on the life raft of emotional extremes, on the crest of the waves one day and in the valley the next. There were no moorings to your faith.

Perhaps in turning from religion you are finding life more and more of a strain. You may be like the high school senior who said, "We are living in the present—tense." Religion is not the sole cause of emotional extremes, neither is it the complete cure. However, you can learn a realistic approach by studying the healthy emotional life of Jesus.

I

In the first place, Jesus had a happy nature. He was friendly and outgoing. In one Scripture passage, we are told that Jesus was talking to the people of his day about the way he could not please them. He contrasted himself with John the Baptist, who was an ascetic. Jesus said that the fasting of John pleased them no less than his own feasting. People called Jesus a glutton and a drunkard. They magnified all out of proportion his enjoyment of parties and good times with people. Jesus took part in the Jewish feasts; he participated in banquets and wedding parties. He liked to be around people when they were having a good time.

You can tell something of Jesus' happy nature by the stories he told. Everyone loved his parables. Children enjoyed listening to his stories, and no doubt they performed little chores about the carpenter's shop just for a chance to hear his fascinating tales. Likewise, adults were fascinated by his stories. His parables were entertaining, and people would listen to them when they would not listen to a lecture on ethics. When the truth dawned on them, the effect was greater than any lecture could produce. He threw the stories out like spiritual hand grenades. People caught them and took them away. Later the truth exploded and became evident. All these stories reveal that they were told by a person who understood the way people lived, not by a hermit but by one who wholeheartedly entered into life.

I vividly recall that my own intensified interest in religion came when I was a junior in high school. I was attracted to a deepened spiritual life by a group of young people who really enjoyed their Christianity. When they sang, "Every day with Jesus is sweeter than the day before," they meant it. They had discovered something of the New Testament idea of Christian fellowship. They enjoyed being together. They felt a guiding purpose in their lives. The enthusiasm on the part of the members of this group was most contagious.

Until recent days the happy nature of Christ has never been emphasized. Not long ago, I read of a man who made a trip around the world, searching for a statue of Christ smiling. He wanted a happy piece of sculpture to place in his garden. His extended search was unsuccessful. Finally, he had to commission a sculptor to do the smiling Christ.

In a Georgia prison an inmate, passing away time, painted a portrait of Christ smiling. When people heard about this they began to send him orders for other portraits of this smiling Christ. He was kept busy painting the unusual pictures.

This happy part of the Master's nature has been magnified as a reaction to the gloomy, late medieval idea of the man of sorrow. Emphasizing either extreme gives you a caricature, however, instead of a portrait of the Master.

You must not forget the dimension of depth in both his happiness and his sorrow.

II

In the second place, Jesus had a serious nature. When he contrasted himself with John the Baptist, he did so in appreciation of the work of the prophetic man. He said to the people, "You have not liked the approach of either of us. One was serious and the other joyful in his presentation of God." But the words of the Master implied that he had immense respect for John the Baptist and his courageous and serious ministry. Perhaps Jesus had in mind a saying of the rabbis. The people mocked at Elijah for his long hair, and they said to Elisha, "Go up thou baldhead."

Jesus did not take his life's mission flippantly; he was deadly serious about trying to be the Saviour of all the people who would accept him as such. He wept over people, because they were as sheep not having a shepherd. Then he shed tears of compassion over the haughty city of Jerusalem, because he had offered the consolation of a mother hen to helpless chicks, and this help they scorned.

Of course, it took a serious view of life for him to face the cross without flinching. He had many opportunities to escape. He might have spoken out in his trials before Pilate and Herod, but he chose the serious strategy of silence. Indeed, he was a "man of sorrows and acquainted with grief," identifying himself with the Suffering Servant described by Isaiah. And when we understand this depth of his personality, we shall know him better as Master and Friend.

There is a solemn joy that goes beyond sad circumstances, like a pile driver seeking solid rock below sandy soil. Such solemnity was evident when President Lincoln wrote this simple letter to Mrs. Bixby in 1864:

I have been shown in the files of the War Department a statement of the adjutant general of Massachusetts that you are the mother of five sons who have died gloriously on the field of battle. I feel how weak and fruitless must be any words of mine which should attempt to beguile you from the grief of a loss so overwhelming. But I cannot refrain from tendering you the consolation that may be found in the thanks of the republic they died to save. I pray that our Heavenly Father may assuage the anguish of your bereavement, and leave you only the cherished memory of the loved and lost, and the solemn pride that must be yours to have laid so costly a sacrifice upon the altar of freedom.[1]

It is encouraging to know that you do not have to face sadness alone. Elizabeth Barrett and Robert Browning had never met, although each was familiar with the published poems of the other. When a mutual friend arranged for them to meet, both looked forward to the interview with keen anticipation. Once they had met each other, their deep friendship and love began. No longer was it just an interest in the published words of the other, but it was an appreciation of personality and a desire to be together. Later she said, "When you came, you never went away."[2] In much the same way, when you come to know Jesus personally, he will stay with you. And when you understand the depth of his seriousness, you will know him better.

Some downward mood swings are to be expected. Often physical weakness and pain combine to cause the collapse of a person's spirits. Even the common cold can cause a sufferer to feel "down in the dumps." Other more serious physical disorders seem to spawn feelings of depression. After surgery, especially the amputation of a limb or the removal of reproductive organs, there is a changed self-concept that frequently leads to melancholy. Following childbirth or upon entering the middle phase of life, a woman often experiences some depressive feelings. In all of these times there is a temptation to withdraw from people, but that is the worst possible response to this mood swing. If the mildly depressed person can get interested in other people and their lives, it will be extremely helpful in pulling him up.

Perhaps here is the secret of Jesus' serious nature, which never descended to the depths of melancholy. He kept his mind on the motive of his life—to help others. He had no time for self-pity, because he went about doing good. He was serious but never depressed.

Another thing to remember when you are depressed is the fact that the mood is temporary. When you are blue and down in the dumps, it seems that this mood has come upon you as a permanent condition for the rest of your life. You might as well ask on a drizzly, dreary day if the rain will last forever. Experience teaches you that the rain is only temporary. The mood is also temporary, lasting a short time and finally passing away. If a feeling of depression should last longer than several days, you should talk with a minister or a psychiatrist about it.

The despondent person usually feels that he is the only one who has ever suffered in such a way. However, the minister who counsels hears many almost identical stories of depressions and moods. The student of church history reads about many of the outstanding saints going through "dark nights of the soul." Indeed, even the Bible is filled with stories of godly men who despaired. When you know that other people have gone through the same experience and have come out alive, their company should be some comfort to you. Elijah did not stay under the juniper tree, and our Lord did not remain in the Garden of Gethsemane; both went on to high experiences in their careers.

III

After you see that Jesus was both happy and sad, then you come to see the amazing truth that he held all of his emotions in balance. It is not easy to balance two weights on scales, and it is even harder to balance contrasting emotions in the personality. Jesus was sensitive enough to balance happiness and sadness. Thereby he achieved poise and confidence. He held his emotions in a healthy tension, without being tense himself.

He was able to accomplish this feat because he was responsive to every surging impulse of the divine. It was not that he held back from sorrow and joy; he entered into both. He saw that they were related. He yearned for this same kind of response in the people of his time, but they disappointed him. Thus, he spoke to them in this manner:

But how can I show what this generation is like? It is like children sitting in the market-place calling out to their friends, "We played at weddings for you but you wouldn't dance, and we played at funerals and you wouldn't cry!" For John came in the strictest austerity and people say, "He's crazy!"

Then the Son of Man came, enjoying life, and people say, "Look, a drunkard and a glutton—the bosom-friend of the tax-collector and the sinner." Ah, well, Wisdom stands or falls by the way her children behave (Matt. 11:16-19, Phillips).

Jesus was saying that he wanted people to have emotions. There are times when a person should make an emotional response. There are times when a person should make an intellectual response to God's revelations. But one should never be so callous as to make no response to God. I feel sure that God would rather hear a person say "no" than merely to disregard his leadership.

Perhaps you have known unresponsive people. You might have called them cold and withdrawn. However, if you grew to know them better you discovered that they were simply afraid of being hurt.

If we could learn from the Master to enter into life wholeheartedly, we should make progress in achieving the healthy emotional stability that he intends for us.

Everyone has mood swings, from elation to sadness. Only when these go to extremes does the psychiatrist label the case "manic-depressive." The average person can maintain a balance in his life by refusing the luxury of emotional extremes.

Recognize the fact of mingled emotions. Someone jokingly said that mixed emotions are evident when you see your mother-in-law driving off a cliff in your brand new Cadillac.

You may persistently work at the project of achieving emotional stability. The program for the graduation of a nurses' school carried this motto: "We have crossed the bay, but the ocean lies before us." That, too, is typical

of the Christian's attitude. He should guard against giving
up. Emerson once said that a man is a hero, not because
he is braver than anyone else, but because he is braver
ten minutes longer. It is said that Thomas Edison carried
out one thousand experiments before he was able to perfect the electric light bulb. What if he had quit after the
nine hundred and ninety-ninth failure? What if you were
to give up now?

As you work to understand the balance in the life of
Jesus, you can develop the same balance in your own
life. But you will need to see and to overcome despair.
Strangely, the spring of the year is when there are more
suicides than at any other time. Perhaps the person who
is despondent begins to see such a contrast between his
own tired soul and the fresh life of the spring landscape,
and he just gives up in despair.

It was in the month of April that I received a telephone
call from a nurse with whom I had had several counseling
sessions. She had been going through the struggle of trying to decide whether to break up her home or to let her
alcoholic husband return once more. She had needed
someone to talk with, someone to hear her without making
her decisions for her. She decided to accept his apologies
and his promises to do better and take him back. Now
she called to say, "He 'broke over.' He is back in jail."
After a long pause came this: "I don't know what I might
do. Life has no meaning."

She was ready to give up in despair but continued to
talk until she had promised to see me the next day. I
cautioned, "Don't do anything important without calling
me first."

During an interview the next day, she was still depressed. I tried to echo her deep feelings. "For the time being life seems to have lost its meaning for you. Things seem dark, almost hopeless. There have been others who have been through this same feeling and have come out. One of the writers in the Old Testament said, 'Out of the depths have I cried unto thee, O Lord' (Psalm 130:1). Like the psalmist, you can be truthful with God."

Later she told me that that conversation had been a turning point in her life. She went back to work and gradually found meaning in life. What she had done, you see, was to find some balance in her emotions. Her problem was still serious and still depressing; yet with God's help it did not get her down.

In our emotional tensions and fears we can go to him who was touched with the feelings of our infirmities but who mastered them. If we make him our Master, then our lives can be lived out in tense times without becoming tense.

9

Christian Resources
for Meeting Grief

DEATH IS a common word in our newspapers today. You read of children dying of leukemia, of young people being killed in car wrecks, of adults dying of cancer and heart attacks. Then as you read you say, "Well, it couldn't happen to our family." Then it does, and you are woefully unprepared for the process of grief.

You need to face grief. It comes to anyone who takes the risk of loving someone other than himself. It comes whenever there is a separation. There does not have to be a death for you to understand the principles of grief. Young men today are leaving for the armed services. Their wives and mothers are discovering the grief that comes from separation. When young people who have been very much in love "agree to disagree," they learn the lesson of grief. Some type of sorrow will come to most of us in the next few months, and we need to know how to meet it. For some it will be death. The principles are the same for separation as well as death.

But you ask, "What good does it do to think of such a

morbid subject?" The answer is that there are Christian resources which are available for use. You need to know of them. Grief can never be eliminated, but it can be gloriously met with the Christian resources that are at your disposal. You need to recognize in advance all the means of invisible support, because you will need to use each one when the time comes.

I

Before you look elsewhere, you can find resources for meeting sorrow within yourself. God has marvelously created you, and he has given you a balance in life. But he has given you powers for maintaining that balance even when the forces of life tend to tilt you over.

You can realize the true resources within yourself only when you refuse the substitutes that are also there. The most common substitute attitude in meeting death is that of false bravery. Some people try to maintain the calm of the Stoics when death comes; they believe in shedding no tears. They want to make a show of being brave at such an hour. To accomplish this feat, they usually repress the memories that try to come back to them. A person of this type will refuse to let the image of the deceased person come into his mind. But when he represses that memory, it is like trying to hold the lid on a pot of boiling water. The steam will get out one way or the other. Likewise, the sorrow will come out in one way or another—if not in tears, maybe in fussing or in a physical illness.

Another substitute for facing sorrow is to turn to something else for relief. Some people turn to excessive drinking. Others turn compulsively to losing themselves in work. Others bury themselves in seclusion. Some turn to keeping a fruitless vigil at the grave.

You can discover the resources that are available within yourself when you admit the feelings within yourself that are common to all people in sorrow. The very first emotion that strikes the heart of the bereaved person is that of extreme loss and pain. This is always accompanied by some expression of grief—often severe sobbing. Yet many times men are frustrated at this very point; they feel that it is unmanly to cry, and they stifle any expression of their sorrow.

When news of President John F. Kennedy's assassination was flashed to the world from Dallas, Texas, people were horrified. From Capitol hill to country crossroads, men began to show signs of grief. This leader, who had become intimately known through the medium of television, was lost to them. The nation grieved like a child for a deceased father.

Few men were able to hold back their tears when the flag-draped coffin arrived at the Capitol, after the muffled drum march from the White House. Before the coffin was moved up the stairs and into the great rotunda, the band gave a flourish and played the triumphant march, "Hail to the Chief." This victorious song was strangely appropriate as the body of the President returned for its final trip to those familiar halls. Because of the intense emotions involved, no one considered it unmanly to cry.

Augustine, that mighty Christian of the fourth century, felt extreme loss and sorrow at the death of his mother. Yet he felt that it was not the Christian thing to mourn. Thus, as he expressed it, his mind commanded his eyes to drink up their fountain wholly dry. Later he realized the folly of this course of action, and he admitted his extreme loss to God and cried alone.

You feel a sorrow at the death of a loved one because your pattern of life is changed. The closer the relationship, the more the routine will be different. When the house grows suddenly quiet and you sit alone, you realize that the pattern of your life is changing. All of the interaction of personalities that had gone before is gone—except in memory. Thus death is always a shock and an adjustment. But this again is a feeling common to all who mourn.

Negative feelings are common to every person in sorrow. These are the most painful to admit. It is hard to admit that the one who died was not perfect and that you had some negative feelings toward him. But if you can recognize that hostility for what it was worth, then you are that much better off. Rabbi Joshua Liebman, the author of *Peace of Mind*, said that admitting this hostility is one of the basic laws in working out grief's slow wisdom.[1]

Another negative feeling that accompanies hostility is guilt. Sometimes the guilt comes because of the feeling of hostility that must be recognized. Then many people are not sure that they took advantage of the opportunities and did enough for the one who is gone. If you can admit these feelings, then you will be doing yourself a favor. You will be preparing to accept the resources which are available.

After any death, but especially after a suicide, there are strong feelings of guilt that need to be expressed.

Sometimes a wife will say, "If only I had not gone to work today, this might not have happened." The husband may say, "If I had just hidden my gun." Friends and relatives may think, "If I had just recognized feelings of despondency and recommended psychiatric care, this might not have happened." These and similar thoughts will be on the minds of the people attending the funeral.

When I conduct a service of this type, I admit that there is a community guilt. I try to express the feelings of all in words such as these: "Yes, there is something more that we could have done. Each one of us has failed in some degree. But we are only human, and we must admit our lack of perfect knowledge. We must admit our guilt altogether and confess it to our merciful Lord."

Another feeling that every bereaved person feels is expressed in the ever-recurring question, "Why has it happened to me?" At some time or other every sorrower questions why God let the tragedy happen to him. But if he admits this feeling and thinks about it, he will soon realize that he is not alone in the matter. Every person who is born into this world will be taken out of it. Death is universal, and you must not feel persecuted when it comes to your family. Oftentimes this feeling causes you to doubt God's goodness or even his existence. But if you recognize that this feeling exists and know that it will soon pass away, you will discover another resource within yourself for meeting grief.

II

There are several resources within the Christian community for meeting grief. Perhaps the first one to be mentioned is the Christian pastor. You can talk with him about your grief. You can express all your doubts and negative feelings, and you can know that he understands. You can know also that he represents a loving God to you. You should talk with him several times in the weeks that follow. And this talking with him is not to be discounted as unimportant. When you really express all you feel to a sympathetic and understanding person, you will find that your talking will dull the edge of the sharp pain of bereavement.

Once I talked with a lady who was a patient in the hospital. She was suffering with her grief problem more than from anything physical. She welcomed an opportunity to talk with a minister. Her sixteen-year-old son had been accidentally killed on the rifle range at a Scout camp. She talked at length about his soul's condition. She was not sure that he was saved, although he had been brought up in the church. Of course, I was not able to tell her if he was or was not. But I listened and helped her talk through the problem, and she arrived at her own conclusion. "He went to the pastor's instruction class. Although he did not join the church, he trusted God. I believe he had his own little private chapel down in his heart." We talked together three times before she left the hospital. During that time she brought out problems of guilt and the readjustment to life. I said little, and I doubt if anything I actually said helped her. But I know that my presence there as one of God's servants helped her tremendously.

Christian friends are a very valuable resource for helping you to face grief. They can also bear the responsibility of listening. It is easier to get over a sudden death if you explain the cause and circumstances over and over to friends as they come. This repetition helps you to accept the shock and realize the reality. Then during the long days of bereavement that follow, the blessing of Christian friends can by their presence and love help you to bear the sorrow, for they will share it with you. How wonderful it is to have a Christian friend come and sit quietly with you and then add before leaving, "I know just what you are going through; I have been through it myself."

In the time of readjustment friends are especially valuable, for they offer new relationships. Every bereaved person should establish new friendships and deepen old ones. This suggestion is not to imply that anyone could ever take the place of the departed one, but you can find a new security and a new satisfaction in being accepted by new friends. The single role formerly held by the deceased can be partially divided among friends.

It is a splendid way of readjustment to life to become active in small groups. It gives you a sense of belonging and significance. Small church groups can challenge you with a goal to meet—some real work of significance and value. Taking an active part in church work can bring new meaning to your life. You can see a dull life become radiant in some type of Christian service.

A pastor in Louisville said to me, "I have two assistant pastors." I looked at him in surprise, for I knew only one was on the staff. Then he said, "The other one is our church visitor, who does her splendid work without one bit of pay." Her husband had been treasurer of the church and had died suddenly. She felt an utter loss and futility in life until the minister suggested that he would like to have her make some calls for him. She politely refused, saying she had never done it before. The minister insisted and made a call with her to show her how it was done. Then she took over. Today she visits at the hospitals every morning and in the homes in the afternoons. She does a marvelous work for the church, but she is quick to tell you that this work has remade her life.

A similar theme is expressed in a play based on Browning's poem, "The Ring and the Book." The young priest in that story had tried hard to prevent a greedy count from murdering his own young wife, Pompilia. The priest had failed to rescue the girl, and she died in his arms. But the wise pope in the drama directed the youthful clergyman from his grief to new fields of service:

> As you led her so others shall you lead,
> Make the world better, show in God's behalf
> That broad brow that reverberates the truth,
> And flash the word God gave you back to man.[2]

Another source of comfort can be found in Christian books. Books by perceptive ministers and laymen have excellent suggestions in them for meeting sorrow. Of course, the Bible is the perennial classic for giving solace. It is good to find Scripture verses that fit you; use them as spiritual prescriptions. A woman said that she was able to face her husband's funeral with spiritual strength because she kept repeating to herself Paul's phrase, "Christ . . . in me" (Gal. 2:20).

You can find resources within yourself and within the Christian community, but the finest resources of all come from our Lord. In his excellent little book, *The Common Ventures of Life*, Elton Trueblood says that with a firm faith you need no other theological explanations for comfort. You can comfort yourself if you have faith in God.

One of the greatest consolations is to be confident of the faith of the one departed. Augustine found his greatest comfort, after the death of his mother, in the fact that a few days before she got sick she told him she was ready to die. She said to the newly converted Augustine, "I've seen my greatest aim accomplished—to see my son a Christian. Now I could die in peace." These words came back to Augustine again and again, bringing more comfort each time they recurred.

If the faith of the deceased has not been that evident, then the efforts of the mourners will often be more frantic to find some straw to which to cling. John Gunther is the author of many best sellers. He is not a religious man himself, but he takes an obvious pleasure in reproducing a prayer his son wrote just before his death. The situation was that his sixteen-year-old son was found to have a brain tumor, with no chance to live. In hope of stirring up some religious sentiment within the boy, the mother began to read him some prayers from all the religions: Hindu, Chinese, Jewish, and Christian. Then the son wrote what he called an "Unbeliever's Prayer." In his book about the boy, Gunther reproduced this prayer:

Almighty God
forgive me for my agnosticism;
For I shall try to keep it gentle, not cynical,
nor a bad influence.

And O! if Thou art truly in the heavens,
accept my gratitude
for all Thy gifts
and I shall try
to fight the good fight. Amen.*

Jesus said to his disciples, "If I go, I will return again unto you." And he promised them the Comforter. He will also return to you as the comforting Holy Spirit. Through his indwelling presence, you can discover spiritual strength you did not know you had. How often you hear people say after a period of mourning, "I just didn't see how I could go through with it, but I found the strength." Jesus gives that strength.

A final divine resource is that of eternal life. God has assured us that this life is not the end. There is at death a releasing into the realm of the eternal. You can find comfort in knowing that the departed Christian is his fullest self now, and that you will join him in Christ's presence someday. Do not mistake the reality of death for the finality of death.

A young man facing the death of his noble Christian mother recalled a quotation she liked, "Death is not extinguishing the light. It is putting out the lamp because the dawn has come."

My grandmother frequently quoted 2 Timothy 4:7-8, and this comforting selection was used at her funeral:

I have fought a good fight, I have finished my course, I have kept the faith: Henceforth there is laid up for me a crown of

---

*"Unbeliever's Prayer," by John Gunther, Jr., from *Death Be Not Proud* by John Gunther, copyright 1949. Reprinted with the permission of Harper & Row, Publishers, Inc.

righteousness, which the Lord, the righteous judge, shall give me at that day: and not to me only, but unto all them also that love his appearing.

10

A Reasonable View
of Divine Healing

THE GOSPELS report thirty-four miracles of healing, and people ask, "Do these things occur today?" The subject of divine healing captures the imagination of the average believer.

The Christian of the space age will do well to refrain from taking extreme attitudes concerning healing. He should avoid the danger of nonbelief in this sophisticated era. When the scientist snickers at the idea of faith healing, the layman should beware of conforming to the image of space-age cynicism.

On the other hand, he should avoid the dangers of a naive acceptance of the idea. A doctor who worked in one of the tuberculosis hospitals in Kentucky told of a patient who, according to all the tests, positively had the disease. Like many other TB patients, this woman had no pain. A religious healer visited the woman and had prayer with her; the healer pronounced her cured. Then her doctor said to her, "We hope you are cured, but we want to test you." He found that the bacillus was still present, but the gullible woman chose to believe the healer. Consequently, she called herself cured by prayer and left the hospital to spread the TB germs wherever she went.

The modern Christian must choose from the divergent views offered by television and tent meeting healers, Christian Science, psychiatrists, and reports from study committees from various denominations.

I

During three years as a hospital chaplain, I met many sick people who claimed that they had been healed of previous troubles. Typical was the person who said of his present illness, "If God healed me previously, why doesn't he do it now?"

Some of these patients came to defeating answers. One said, "God is far away from me now." Thus, at a time when he needed a refuge, a strength, a very present help in time of need, he lost touch with God and clasped hands with disillusionment. Emphasis on physical healing may produce many unwholesome attitudes.

While studying clinical pastoral care, I noticed an accident victim with a dirty cloth tied around his head. The scene contrasted sharply with the spotlessly clean hospital. One of the interns reported that the man's mother had been to a tent meeting; she had purchased a cloth blessed by the healer, and she had tied it around the head of her injured son. I was interested in finding out more about the healer. I attended a service, and I shall never forget the scene I saw that night. Near the stage was an assortment of people on cots, stretchers, and in wheelchairs. They had come to the meeting hoping for healing, and almost all of them returned no better. They had seen a few favored ones receive miraculous cures, but they themselves left the tent, dragging added burdens of despondency.

Another negative feeling that often accompanies physical healing is pride. There is a strange reaction that often occurs when a person gets better. He seldom says, "Look what God did for me." Usually he says, "Look what my faith has accomplished." And so divine healing has come to be known as "faith" healing, not so much dependent on God's power as upon man's faith.

The New Testament is specific in warning against strange teachings. Jesus said that his followers could recognize a person by his fruits. Paul, who prayed for physical healing and was denied it, warned young Christians to avoid profane and old wives' tales. Thus, in the Christian spirit of testing, you may ask the following questions about a faith healer:

1. Is the healer sincere? Is he humble?

2. Does he claim that his is the only method of healing, disregarding the trained work of doctors and nurses?

3. Does he emphasize other parts of the gospel, such as righteous living and the importance of eternal life?

4. Is the "cure" a lasting one?

The last question reminds me of a little boy who had had polio. He had received expert treatment from a hospital in Louisville, and he had been advised to wear braces on his weakened legs. His mother took him to a healing meeting at which he was pronounced cured. He was told to take off the braces and walk across the stage. Under the excitement of the moment, he did just that. But the next day his legs seemed weaker than ever, and he found

out that he would have to put on the braces again. I
have not worried about the people at that meeting who
were convinced that they had seen another miraculous
cure, but I have been concerned about what impression
that little boy received of God. What could he possibly
think of a Lord who would forget about him during three
hundred sixty-four days of the year but suddenly,
in a big crowd of people, grant him a twenty-four-hour
favor? I am afraid that he received a disappointing and
an unreal view of God.

This discussion would not attempt to limit God's power.
Every minister has been called in upon a case in which a
doctor said, "I have done everything I can. Now it is in
the Lord's hands." Then during anxious hours of crisis,
the minister and family quietly offered up confident
prayers for healing. The patient began to improve, and
pastor and people were grateful to the doctor and to the
Lord. They became convinced that God worked through
reasonable and natural means, using the disciplines of
medical science but going beyond that skill. Wise was the
physician who said, "I dress the wounds; it is God who
heals."

II

Once you recognize the negative aspects of physical
healing, then you see that spiritual healing is more important. Two Scriptures indicate that the two ideas cannot be separated from each other. Note, however, that the
spiritual deserves the greater emphasis. The psalmist had
profound insight when he prayed, "Lord, be merciful unto
me: heal my soul; for I have sinned against thee" (Psalm

41:4). Likewise, the words which Jesus chose as the text of his inaugural address show a depth of understanding: "He hath sent me to bind up the broken-hearted" (Isa. 61:1).

A further contrast of the supremacy of the spiritual over the physical is seen in the frustrated prayer of Paul. He was a man of courageous character and deep faith. Thus, he prayed for divine healing that he might become an even better servant of the Lord. His prayer was answered, but the answer was no. Then in one of the classic expressions of Paul, the old missionary reports on God's answer to his request and his own reaction to it. "He said unto me, My grace is sufficient for thee: for my strength is made perfect in weakness. Most gladly therefore will I rather glory in my infirmities, that the power of Christ may rest upon me" (2 Cor. 12:9).

Praying for health is like praying for money. There is always a selfish element in the prayer. God has given no assurance that the Christian should be healthier or richer than anyone else. However, God has assured the Christian that he will be with him in times of sickness and in times of poverty.

One of the high points in *The Robe* by Lloyd Douglas was the conversation that the seeking soldier had with the girl Miriam. Here was a lovely girl who was still an invalid, although she had seen the Saviour and come to know him. She gladly told the soldier who was seeking for some meaning in his life the answer she had found to her own life's search. Jesus had not healed her physically, but he had healed her spiritually. She had been a carping and grumbling invalid; Jesus made her loving and forgiving. That was a greater miracle.

Jesus dealt with disturbed people. Many of the people he ministered to were ones with deep emotional conflicts. Many of those same ones, if living today, would be receiving treatment in mental hospitals. Many of the patients who came to the Great Physician were ones weighted down with the burden of guilt and the anxiety of dying. Jesus gave them release from that old way of life and granted them a new being. His forgiveness produced in them courage for facing life victoriously.

Jesus was able to bring healing to these people because they brought to him the shattered resources of their lives. Jesus, who brought reconciliation into the world, applied this reconciliation specifically to divided personalities. Paul Tillich, in *The New Being*, describes what these people received from the Christ:

They surrendered their persons, split, contradicting themselves, disgusted and despairing about themselves, hateful of themselves and therefore hostile towards everybody else; afraid of life, burdened with guilt feelings, accusing and excusing themselves, fleeing from others into loneliness, fleeing from themselves to others, trying finally to escape from the threats of existence into the painful and deceptive safety of mental and bodily disease. As such beings they surrendered to Jesus and this surrender is what we call faith.[1]

III

When you look closer at the healing that is called divine, you see that it is a total healing. God does not treat you as a soul and a body; he offers his love to you as a son, a total being. Therefore, God is able to bring healing to the total personality and body.

A healing that comes from God does not have to be sudden to be miraculous. It usually takes many months for a patient under the care of a psychiatrist to work out a healthy approach to life. That healing comes from God. It takes a long time for broken bones to knit back. But that healing, too, comes from the forces of nature, specifically from God himself.

I would like to describe for you a case that I consider true divine healing. A young woman of twenty-six years had been unable to walk for the last thirteen years, exactly half of her life. The dreaded paralyzer, polio, had made her legs useless at the age of thirteen, and she had used a wheelchair since then.

One night during a religious service in a little Baptist church in Kentucky, she felt that she had a definite Christian task to accomplish. She felt very close to God. (Now you are expecting me to say that she got up and walked out of that meeting. No, God seldom works his will in that way.) She felt an assurance in her heart that she would one day walk again, and that assurance was the beginning of the miracle.

Her family discouraged her. Her aging family doctor told her that walking was a medical impossibility. Still undaunted, she told her hopes to a young dentist. He referred her to a young specialist who was developing some new techniques in this field. This surgeon agreed to operate on her legs, to restore to usefulness the tendons in her heels. God can work through trained people.

In the hospital she found one verse in the book of Psalms that brought her comfort. It spoke to her condition: "Teach me thy way, O Lord; I will walk in thy truth:

unite my heart to fear thy name" (Psalm 86:11). She seized the words "I will walk" out of their context, and she held on to them with Christian hope.

After the operation she was sent to a rehabilitation center, where many others in similar conditions were receiving gradual help in adjusting to more productive lives. She received braces for her legs. She received stimulation in the unused legs through hot baths and physical therapy. She received a pair of crutches, and she was taught the principles of walking by a trained teacher. Although her walking is slow, because of the crutches and braces, it is sure. Her heart dances for joy. This young woman said to me, her chaplain, "My walking is a miracle. A year ago I wouldn't have thought it possible. And it is due to the help of so many, many people. But the credit goes to God."

11
Take Atheism Seriously

THE SUPREME COURT ruling which outlawed required Bible reading and prayer in public schools was not intended to encourage atheism; it simply defined the state's relationship to religion as neutral. However, the atheists who led in the legal fight have been encouraged by the ruling, which they refer to as their "victory." Recently, they announced aggressive plans to establish a university, library, printing plant, radio station, auditorium for seminars, and a home for aged atheists.

Many of us in this country are too complacent about the religious life of America. We are overconfident about the *faith* of our fathers, and we forget about the possible outright *atheism* of their grandchildren.

Christians should study atheism, just as a physician studies cancer. One of the largest training centers for church workers in the world recently established a department of atheism. Courses are to be offered to mature students to help them understand godlessness wherever it appears.

Americans need to recognize the disease of atheism. We need to study the causes and then to offer a cure. We must take atheism seriously.

I

What makes one an atheist? The average person meets so few atheists in his lifetime that he considers an atheist to be one who has sat down and thought and concluded that there is no God. Yet it is not really that simple. An atheist does a lot of thinking, but that thinking is shaped by his experiences.

A psychologist will tell you that usually an atheist is a person who has no close ties with an earthly father. Sometimes a baby born out of wedlock grows up to have no confidence in a father and, therefore, becomes an atheist. Sometimes, in another instance, a child will see a dominating, ugly-tempered father beat the mother and then desert the family in order to have no worries, and he despises the name "father." The psychologist can show you that many times these children who have had no close ties with an earthly father cannot understand the meaning of a Heavenly Father. This is not to say that every child who has had the traumatic experience of losing a father becomes an atheist, because many do not. However, many who are atheists have had this deprivation in their background.

Some seem to cultivate atheism merely for the value it has in shocking people. Perhaps a person wants to surprise his friends and be a different type of person in college. Or, perhaps a young person wants to break with strict authoritarian parents, and so he disavows their God.

Once I talked with a young woman who had done this very thing. Her mother was strict in her religion, almost to the point of being a fanatic. The girl had had an undependable father. In college she came across ideas of communism and atheism, and she embraced those ideas. I felt sorry for her because of her cynicism, and she felt sorry for me. She said something that reflected her whole attitude of disillusionment and willingness to shock. "I think ministers are a useless ornament in society; they are like the cigarette girl in the night club. She is there, not to perform any real service, but simply to make the place a little more attractive."

Some have turned to atheism simply because they have been disillusioned with belief and idealism. They have studied the lives of believers; they have seen the activities of the church. They have found nothing in these to recommend a continued belief. Therefore, they have given up their ideas. A mature minister, Harry Emerson Fosdick, made the following remark about the disillusionment of a famous atheist at the turn of the century:

Ingersoll represents a tragedy, repeated innumerable times in my day—a man with the makings of a good Christian, in some of his attitudes and activities displaying a more Christian spirit than the average run of churchmen, turned into an atheist by the honest necessity of rebelling against a crude, incredible orthodoxy.[1]

We might class these people with ones who have turned to atheism because of an emotional response, and yet there are some who have turned to atheism because of an intellectual response. Over the years there have been many scholarly and honest people who felt that traditional Christianity did not offer an answer to the world's problems. These include such names as Voltaire, Rousseau, Herbert Spencer, and the modern French existentialists. Most of these have turned to a naturalistic explanation of the universe.

Then there are those who are disturbed by the problem of evil. A modern philosopher, Karl Jaspers, says that any honest man is so revolted and repelled by the tragedy of life that he is tempted to deny God or to rebel against existence. His statement sounds almost like a summary of the book of Job. That poor, despicable man of the Old Testament fought a battle within his soul. Once he cried out, "Oh that I knew where I might find him!" (Job 23:3).

The same struggle of the soul is evident in the following prayer letter from an attorney in St. Louis. This man, Lee Meriwether, was born during the Civil War. His mother, a southern woman, was deeply afraid of the Union forces that were occupying the South. She passed along to the child some of the resentment that she had.

Dear God:
   If you really exist somewhere in the endless space of the universe and have power to grant or deny men's prayers, please grant this prayer of mine. . . .
   Please kill the Devil, or at any rate prevent him from continuing his wicked work.
   Some of the men you create are as savage as jungle beasts; four years ago cannibals in South America killed and ate the missionaries trying to teach them to adore you. Please don't create more cannibals.
   You who know the Present and the Past also know the Fu-

ture, please don't create men you know will be so evil that they will be put in hell.

Dear God, I have never prayed to you because I have never been able to believe you exist: if I am mistaken please forgive me and grant this, the only prayer I have ever said.

Respectfully,
Lee Meriwether[2]

The courage, honesty, and pathos of this unbeliever's prayer seem to indicate that he is not too distant from the kingdom itself.

There is also the atheism of indifference. You and I very seldom meet a person who will admit that he is an atheist, but we have many people around us who act like atheists. These are people with a "couldn't-care-less" attitude toward religion. In a world that demands decisions, they remain unconcerned. Paul Tillich says that atheism means "to remain unconcerned about the meaning of one's existence. Indifference toward the ultimate question is the only imaginable form of atheism."[3]

II

Now that we have seen some of the factors that make an atheist, let us see what the Christian can do about it. First of all, he can strengthen the foundation of his own beliefs. He can look deep into the recesses of his soul, or he can peer far back into the fog of prehistoric times. The answer he finds in either place is the same that is found in the first verse of the Bible, "In the beginning God created the heaven and the earth." These are mysterious and magnificent words. They have been challenged by many people, but they have never been disproved.

More diligently than the Communist nations are teaching atheism, let us teach about God. Let us improve our home life. Fathers, behold your calling. Do not seek havens of escape from your family. Rather, see your children as companions and work with them. Stay in your garden, with your children helping you, instead of making a vacation trip hundreds of miles away from your family. Stay at home and enjoy some leisure time. Learn to laugh with them again. Teach them a true meaning of a father's love and forgiveness, in order that they might understand God's love and forgiveness.

Likewise, let us improve our church life. Let the church stand for something. Let it take seriously the criticism that the world is making. Let us recall the words of the Communist girl. She talked of the pastor as a social figure. Let the church be a schoolroom for Christian living. The church could also be a laboratory for the transformation of neighborhoods everywhere.

This suggestion brings us to improving community life. By what reasoning do we conclude that religion is a private affair between a person and his own spiritual "pen pal"? The New Testament teaches, "Pure religion and undefiled before God and the Father is this, To visit the fatherless and widows in their affliction, and to keep himself unspotted from the world" (James 1:27).

Let us improve not only home life, church life, community life; let us also improve national life. Let us send to Washington only the best representatives of Christian character America can produce. Let us recommend to the Peace Corps only the finest examples of God-fearing young men and women who can take a spiritual message at the same time that they are carrying a democratic message to other nations of the world.

Billy Graham says,

We should convey the fact to the Russian people that although we strongly dislike their Communism and detest wholeheartedly their political philosophy, as a people we love them, we pray for them, we long for them to experience the liberty, happiness, prosperity and faith which we enjoy.[4]

When you see a man out on a limb, sawing the limb off, you rush to warn him. We need to make haste in warning a large section of the world that in its godless overconfidence it is heading for oblivion.

During a recent trip behind the Iron Curtain, an American youth leader was told by a mother that her little girl came home from school her first day with an atheistic indoctrination. The child said, "I learned today that all those things you have been telling me about Jesus are just fairy tales."

Also it was reported to him that in the schools they ask the children to pray for cookies. They look up from their prayers and see nothing. Then with heads bowed again, they are asked to pray to the Communist state for cookies. Then, in a diabolical scheme, someone comes in the door with a large plate of cookies to hand out. Day in and day out the schools are now teaching that there is no God.

Despite all these things, I do not despair. I believe that the force of God is so strong within the human heart that some of the indoctrinated children will throw aside their atheism. They will find it unrealistic and not suitable for a world of turmoil that demands a faith that will stand up

in these times. I have a feeling that there will be more
and more people all over the world who have once tried
communism, but who have found it to be an idolatry that
failed. I believe these people will once again turn toward
the only true God, our Creator.

> Truth, crushed to earth shall rise again,
>   The eternal years of God are hers;
> But Error, wounded, writhes in pain,
>   And dies among his worshippers.
>
> WILLIAM CULLEN BRYANT

Prayer: O Lord, as thou hast kept America free, now
keep her true. As thou hast kept her rich, now make her
good. Amen.

12

The Five Steps in Repentance

WHO CAN ever forget the teasing laugh, the sugary voice, and the dazzling beauty of Marilyn Monroe? These characteristics, emphasized by make-up artists, hair stylists, and press agents, built her into a star of the first magnitude, a personality known all over the world.

She symbolized our times. She achieved everything that the world considers worth struggling to attain. Yet underneath her tight-fitting evening gown, she was simply an insecure little orphan dressed in a pinafore. A national magazine stated that guilt was her constant companion. The things she lived for were not enough to keep her living. She never solved the problem of her conscience, it seems. Thus, she tossed aside fame and fortune with an overdose of sleeping pills.

There are many other people not so famous, carrying burdens of guilt far too heavy for a mortal to bear. There are some lying awake at night, staring at the ceiling, enduring a restless sadness down deep in the heart. There

are many sinners who need to understand the steps in
repentance.

The Bible indicates that there are five steps in repentance. These steps go beyond simply feeling sorry,
because the human soul is not that simple. Repentance is
a complicated matter. It is a grave matter, not to be
ignored or considered lightly. You can learn much from
David in his discovery of these steps in repentance.

I

Releasing sorrow is the first step in repentance. David
was a man of bottled-up sorrow. Ruling from a throne of
absolute power, he gave orders and people obeyed. He
was not in the habit of apologizing, nor of seeking anyone's forgiveness. He did just as he pleased, and it pleased
him on one occasion to take another man's wife and send
that man to the front line in battle for certain death. Sub-
sequently, the king did not dare to reveal to others the
guilt he felt, for this admission would seem a weakness in
his strong character.

When sitting as a judge, his mind wandered from the
case. He seemed preoccupied. When servants marched in
from the kitchen, bearing his favorite foods served on gold
and silver platters, he was not hungry. He bellowed to
them to get it out of his sight.

The king was absent-minded, down in the dumps, and
irritable because he had never let any sorrow for his sins
come to the surface. He admitted no remorse. He was
like a soldier who receives a serious wound across the
brow. His mind is on the battle, and he does not guess that
blood is oozing down his forehead. It takes someone else

to notice his condition and to point out the wound to him. To perform this task, God sent his prophet, a little old man called Nathan.

Nathan was a man skilled in the knowledge of human nature. He had something of that same quality that was so evident in the personality of Jesus. Both men understood people's problems, and they told simple stories to make the people come to understand their own problems. They did not spoil the effectiveness of their work by condemning.

The prophet began spinning a web of words. He described a rich man with many flocks and a poor man with one little lamb. The poor farmer loved the little lamb like a member of the family; he even let it eat from his plate and drink from his cup. But the rich man wanted the little pet to make some lamb stew, and he arrogantly seized it.

David intently listened to the dramatic story. He became more angered all the while. Finally, he beat his fist on a table and exclaimed, "That man is worthy of death." The word "death" echoed out into the courtyard of the royal palace.

Quietly and firmly, the short prophet said, "You are the man." For a moment, the king was speechless. Then a moan escaped his lips. Like the fighting soldier, advised of his wounded condition, David realized the serious condition of his soul. Now he could grieve over it. He bowed his head in shame at the foolishness of his actions. He regretted that he had been so arrogant as to make his own rules for living and to disregard God's eternal laws. For the first time King David was facing the sorrow of his experience.

Many people are living today in the shadows of sin. They do not find any forgiveness, because they have never taken the first step in God's direction, and that step is sorrow. Frequently when you talk with a person in jail, he says, "I am sorry for all of this." What he means is that he is sorry that he got caught, but he is still unrepentant in the depths of his soul.

A Jewish philosopher says this: "He who is dominated by the idol that he wishes to win, to hold, and to keep—possessed by a desire for possession—has no way to God but that of reversal, which is a change not only of goal but also of the nature of the movement."[1] This reversal is the beginning of repentance. It continues by seeking to be possessed of God—not by trying to possess him.

II

The next step is confession. The noble David could not sit in silence and listen to the voice of Nathan recounting his sins. Neither could he sit inactive as his conscience whispered louder and louder. In a hoarse voice, he replied, "I have sinned against the Lord."

Although a man's life had been taken and a woman's honor ruined, David still said, "I have sinned against the Lord." Any sin is against the holy, pure, and righteous God Almighty. David had done more than break the commandments against murder and against adultery. He had started off by putting other gods before him, and he had ended up by coveting. God's law meant nothing to him at the time of his defection, and now he realizes the seriousness and the blackness of his sins.

We have often made the mistake of confessing our little

misdeeds and forgetting the deeper attitudes of the soul.
A friend of mine in the Navy was a devout Catholic. One
day after lunch he suddenly said to me, "I have got to go
to the priest and confess. I had forgotten today is Friday,
and I have just eaten a hamburger."

A similar experience in triviality is common to all of us
Protestants. A Christian psychologist says this about the
confessing person:

The superficial deeds which he remembers can be easily told
and are easily plucked, but these are only the poisonous flowers blossoming above the earth. The roots remain in the unconscious, and they will thrive again and again—new flowers,
new sins to be confessed daily.[2]

The poisonous roots must be pulled up by the painful
method of real confession.

A man hits his thumb with a hammer and says something harmless. A woman skips a page in a book for which
she requests church credit. A person neglects a tithe one
Sunday or misses attending a worship service one week
on vacation. Then he picks out this minor misdeed to confess and overlooks the serious disorders of his soul.

You must deal with sin as with a weed in your garden.
You cannot leave it alone. A wise preacher said,

No man's sin ever is done with until it has come through this
process of forgiveness. Either your sin has been forgiven or
else it is yet in you as sin. I think this is about the solemnest
fact in human life. . . . Go down into that secret place. Unlock
that hidden door. Take out that unforgiven sin. For your soul's
sake, get rid of it! But there is only one way. Whatever theology you hold, it is the way of the cross—penitence, confession, restitution, pardon.[3]

III

The next step is restitution, a strange and uncomfortable word for modern ears. Can you imagine what would happen today if a preacher were to refuse to accept for membership a wealthy and influential politician because he had a reputation for dishonesty? If he said, "No, come back after you have given evidence of a cleaned up life," many members would be horrified. Yet these words are biblical.

John the Baptist set the example for saying no. Curiosity seekers and crowd conformists went out to the Jordan banks to hear him speak. They left their humdrum activities in town to participate in the excitement of the baptismal services. Yet John called the crowd "snakes in the grass." He shouted to the Pharisees and publicans, "Bring forth therefore fruits worthy of repentance" (Luke 3:8). Giving evidence of repentance is scriptural.

This third step in repentance is often overlooked. But when a truly penitent sinner acts on it, then he will prove to himself and to the world what God already knows— that he is sincere in thirsting for forgiveness.

When you recall the experience of David, you can understand how frustrated he was at this step. In the parable of the lamb, he had ordered that the guilty thief restore four lambs for the one he had seized and killed. If David had stolen a suit of armor, a chest of money, or a prized war horse, he could have returned them. But how could he call from the dead one who had crossed over into that land from which no traveler returns? Although David had pushed Uriah into the river of death, he could not bring

him out again. And what could he do to restore the form-
er condition of sensual Bathsheba? Nothing! David wished
there were something he could do, but he could only
grieve over his sin.

Perhaps your sin is different. Perhaps there is some
money that is burning your pocketbook and always will
until you return it. Perhaps there is some wall of separation you have built, and it can be torn down only by your
apology to a friend or to a member of another race. Perhaps there is some lie that you can retract. Perhaps you
have committed a sin of silence, saying nothing while
your church was criticized. In any of these sins, you can restore, and you can help to make up for your wrongdoing.
A person who has spent forty years without Christ can
make up for that vacuum by working for him the next
forty.

IV

The next step in repentance is pardon. Until a gift is
accepted, it cannot be enjoyed. God offers his pardon to
the penitent heart; but until that person actually realizes
the pardon, he cannot enjoy a release from his guilt.

It was a great relief for David to hear the words of
assurance, "The Lord also hath put away thy sin; thou
shalt not die" (2 Sam. 12:13). The forgiven king began to
relax in God's love. He knew that he would not be killed
as a punishment. And we know that the prophet's words
meant he would not have to die eternally.

Frequently a pastor hears the pleading question, "Is it
possible for God to forgive me after all I have done?"
When I am talking with such a person in an intimate

relationship of counseling, I do not answer in my words but in the words of the Scriptures: "If we confess our sins, he is faithful and just to forgive us our sins, and to cleanse us from all unrighteousness" (1 John 1:9).

Likewise, many other people know that God has forgiven them, but they cannot forgive themselves. It is possible for a person to be so strict on himself that he does not realize the joy of forgiveness.

The person who truly confesses is not giving another thought to "next time." If he is conscientious about repenting, he intends to do better. Thus, God, in forgiving him of sin, shows the high expectation that the person will do better at the next opportunity.

There was a young musician in the Royal Band of Hanover. He was a talented musician, but he despised fighting. He left the battlefield of Europe and fled to England. He knew there was a death penalty over his head, but he avoided capture. He loved the stars and became a great astronomer. With patient endeavor he constructed a telescope, with which he scanned the heavens each night. One night he discovered a new planet and became world famous. The king sent for him to come to Windsor Castle. But the king was George of Hanover, whom he had originally deserted. Yet the king sent him a royal pardon. "Now," said the king, "we can talk, and you shall live at Windsor and be Sir William Herschel."[4] In a very similar way, God forgives the sinner and then makes him a son.

V

Receiving pardon is not the final step in repentance. David's experience is similar to all of life. God may forgive his sin, but he does not remove the consequences. David hears the prophet assure him of God's pardon, and then the next word is "howbeit," meaning "however, nevertheless." Life always adds a "however."

Sin brings consequences. Do not call it punishment from an angry God. He could remove these consequences if he performed a miracle for you. However, God has already performed a greater miracle when he has granted you pardon from guilt. The consequences serve as a warning not to relapse.

David discovered sin's consequences. The child of his unlawful union died. Also he found that his family always would be quarreling, and this result was the logical outcome of polygamous relationships. The sons of different mothers could not get along with each other, and their lives ended up tragically. Their country was plunged into civil war as an indirect result.

The consequences of sin are similar to the holes that are left from nails being driven into a piece of wood. God removes the nails of sin from the wood; yet the holes of memory remain. In a similar way, God will heal a deep cut across the forehead. Yet the scar remains. Sin has its consequences, and you can learn from these consequences the will of God in avoiding sin in your new life with him.

It is up to you. No one can repent for you. No one can take the first step for you. There is no need for you to be without the assurance of God's forgiveness. Repentance can be the most important event in your life.

One of the most vivid memories of my life was when I stood by a dying man. He was a twenty-nine-year-old father of four children and a carpenter by trade. He had been laying a hardwood block floor with inflammable glue, when someone dropped a match and everything in the room began to burn. His clothes caught afire, and he ran out screaming and fell in the yard.

A few minutes later I saw him in the hospital emergency room. He was black as a cinder. He was not concerned about his looks, however. Neither was he concerned about his pain. He said to me, "I haven't done right. I want God to forgive my sins." Repentance was the most important thing on his mind.

At this point, his wife dropped to her knees by the bed and started to pray aloud. When she finished I said some words from Psalm 46: "God is our refuge and strength, a very present help in trouble. Therefore will not we fear." And just before he lapsed into unconsciousness, I assured him, "God is near you, and he hears your prayers."

13

The Re-Entry Problem

EXPLORING INNER SPACE puts you into a private orbit of seclusion. As you read about improving and as you spend time in confessional prayer, you are isolated from people. To remain withdrawn would be tragic. You need to re-enter the world of people.

The problem of returning to people was shared by Moses after his burning bush experience. He was a man who had lived in an environment of semi-isolation and who had spent many hours contemplating his past. He was commissioned by his God to return to a people in need of his insights. Moses, who had gazed with wonder on the burning bush and who had approached his God with reverence, had received information that he knew he must share with his people. It was not easy for him, and he put up many excuses.

From the time of Moses to the time of John Glenn, the problem of re-entry has not been easy. The astronaut can tell you that putting a man into orbit is not as much of a problem as getting him back to earth. The re-entry of an astronaut is one of critical danger. Yet when he accomplishes his mission, he brings back a perspective of this world that the rest of us dream about and wish for.

You can see the similarity in your experience with that of Moses and the astronaut. You have gained insight and perspective during this time of reading, this period of withdrawal. The strategic question now is this: Can you engage in a successful re-entry?

You will find it unrealistic to force your newly discovered insight on other people. You can recommend ideas to your friends, but you cannot force insight on them. English grammar is psychologically correct when it says that you can teach someone, but you cannot "learn" him —he must do the learning himself.

I recall that after I had taken a course in pastoral care and had read several books in this field, I was tremendously impressed with the power of the unconscious in our religious life. I was fascinated by a book on prayer titled *The Dazzling Darkness*, written by a canon of the Church of England. The ideas in it were so clear to me that I thought it would be doing others a favor to pass the insights along. When asked to speak in my home church, I named my topic, based on a chapter in this book, "The Coal Mine of Prayer." Nothing could have been of less interest to those people at the First Baptist Church, Jackson, Mississippi, than a discussion on the subconscious prayer life. It was about as appetizing to them as serving wet potato chips. Later a saintly old man said to me, "You didn't preach; you just gave a book review." Experiences like this teach us that we cannot force insight on people.

Another way to use insight incorrectly is with belligerence. What a temptation it is, when you grow angry with a person, to say, "You're just a neurotic." When you have learned the classifications in abnormal psychology, it is a real temptation to try to fit your acquaintances into these slots. How easy it becomes to say, "This guy is a real manic-depressive, if I ever saw one." If you analyze your motives for placing people in these neat categories, you will find that your action is an anxious attempt to build up your own ego. Perhaps you have not mastered that chapter in the Bible that begins with these ideas: "Though I speak with the jargon of psychology and in the slang of the space age, and have not agape [love], I am become as sounding brass, or a tinkling cymbal."

I know of a student who became quite sophisticated in psychological phraseology. With the help of counseling, he became aware of the shortcomings in his personality development. However, he used this knowledge as a weapon against his parents. They were defenseless when he said to them, "You surely made a mess of raising me; I expect to do better with my own children." Those poor parents were vulnerable against such a weapon. It was too late for them to do anything about rearing their son. His statement filled them with disappointment.

The insights from your exploration should not make you self-centered. Dwight L. Moody said, "I have had more trouble with myself than with any other man I have ever met." Being concerned about yourself can be a legitimate interest. But self-concern may be taken to an extreme. Someone once asked, "What is your world's biggest problem?" The student answered, "Me."

Analyzing yourself could lead you to grow more egocentric and self-conscious. This introspection could lead you into all kinds of vanity, until your main occupation would consist of "writing a diary," and your chief interest would lie in becoming a more exceptional case. You could become intemperate with the luxury of solitude. These conditions will come to pass only if your original motive was a selfish one. But if pain, guilt, sorrow, or the love of God drove you to self-examination, then their solution will jar you out of self-centeredness.

Self-improvement sounds like self-salvation. But having been saved by Christ, you are under an obligation to become more Christlike. People who have already received the Holy Spirit are told in 2 Corinthians 7:1, "Let us cleanse ourselves." As someone has said, "The largest room in the world is that for self-improvement."

When you take a few steps along a trail, you do not claim that these conclude the hike. No, they are just the beginning. Similarly, starting an interest in your soul's development will not mean the conclusion to self-knowledge; the interest should stimulate a continuing journey.

At the beginning you discovered a certain determination in your life not to know yourself. You had to admit that you were not in agreement with the words of the psalmist, "Search me, O God, and know my heart: try me, and know my thoughts" (Psalm 139:23). Such words went against your grain, and you probably harbored the following attitudes: "Flee from me, O God. Let me have my own secrets. Do not trouble me and disturb my thoughts. Do not look for evil in my life, because I am doing the best I can. I do not want to know more about myself, and I can make my own way in life." Getting beyond the gravitational pull of such attitudes is just the beginning of inner discovery.

Almost everyone has been to a party and heard the host abruptly announce, "It's time to stop the recorder and play back the tape." Listening to the playback, you declare all the voices sound natural except yours. The reason is that you are not accustomed to hearing yourself. The recorder gives you a different perspective. This same type of perspective in self-discovery is available from God.

A man in the hospital during December noticed that several doctors and nurses passed by his room carrying beautifully wrapped presents. He asked, "Is someone special down the hall?"

The reply came, "They are not carrying the gifts to a patient. You see, the X-ray department is down the hall. They are running their own packages under the fluoroscope to find out what is in them."

The only way you can understand yourself is to use God's X ray. If you have begun its use, continue it. The person who does deserves a medal for spiritual bravery. He is like the cancer patient who said to his surgeon just before surgery, "Cut deep."

The idea of God's intimate knowledge terrifies you and me. We shudder to think that there is one person in all the universe that we have not fooled, one that we have not been able to keep a secret from, one that knows us better than we know ourselves. Yet the brave Christian gives thanks for this thought and prays that God will continually search through his soul to reveal undiscovered parts that need to be staked out and claimed for his kingdom, to be ruled over by the King of kings.

Notes

Chapter 1

1. Frances Winwar, *The Immortal Lovers* (New York: Harper & Bros., 1950), p. 31.
2. "Two Gods," *Masterpieces of Religious Verse*, ed. James Dalton Morrison (New York: Harper & Bros., 1948), p. 12.
3. *The Interpersonal Theory of Psychiatry* (New York: W. W. Norton & Co., 1953), pp. 34, 310.
4. C. D. Meigs, "Others," *The Broadman Hymnal* (Nashville: Broadman Press, 1940), p. 77.
5. Used by permission.

Chapter 2

1. Edward Sandford Martin, "My Name Is Legion," *Masterpieces of Religious Verse*, p. 274.

Chapter 3

1. *Dynamics of Faith* (New York: Harper & Bros., 1957), p. 22.
2. *What Is Vital in Religion* (New York: Harper & Bros., 1955), pp. 92–93.
3. *A Guide to Confident Living* (New York: Prentice-Hall, 1948), p. 137.

Chapter 4

1. Lofton Hudson, *The Christian Index*, August 14, 1958.
2. "The Rock," *The Complete Poems and Plays, 1909–1950* (New York: Harcourt, Brace & Co., 1952), p. 96.
3. (New York: The Ronald Press Co., 1950), p. 153.
4. *Understanding Human Nature* (New York: Garden City Publishing Co., 1927), p. 135.

Chapter 5

1. Charles T. Holman, *Psychology and Religion for Everyday Living* (New York: The Macmillan Co., 1949), p. 81.
2. (New York: Longmans, Green & Co., 1902), p. 181.
3. *Ibid.*, p. 182.
4. *A Second Reader's Notebook*, ed. Gerald Kennedy (New York: Harper & Bros., 1959), p. 349.

Chapter 6

1. "An Infantile Neurosis," *Collected Papers* (New York: Basic Books, 1959), III, 597.
2. L. H. Marshall, *The Challenge of New Testament Ethics* (London: Macmillan & Co., 1948), p. 140.
3. *Ibid.*

Chapter 7

1. Charles M. Schulz, "Peanuts," November 10, 1959. Used by permission.

Chapter 8

1. *The Lincoln Encyclopaedia*, comp. & ed. Archer H. Shaw (New York: The Macmillan Co., 1950), p. 22.
2. Winwar, *op. cit.*, p. 144.

Chapter 9

1. (New York: Simon & Schuster, 1946), pp. 105–133.
2. Arthur F. Goodrich and Rose A. Palmer, *Caponsacchi* (New York: Appleton & Co., 1927), p. 174.

Chapter 10

1. (New York: Charles Scribner's Sons, 1955), pp. 38–39.

Chapter 11

1. *The Living of These Days* (New York: Harper & Bros., 1956), p. 21.

2. *State-Times* (Jackson, Mississippi), January 27, 1961, Sec. A, p. 4.

3. Quoted in J. Claude Evans, "Campus Atheism or Apathy?" *Motive*.

4. *Newsweek* (October 18, 1954), p. 60.

Chapter 12

1. Martin Buber, *I and Thou*, trans. Ronald Gregor Smith (New York: Charles Scribner's Sons, 1957), p. 105.

2. Fritz Kunkel, *In Search of Maturity* (New York: Charles Scribner's Sons, 1943), p. 252.

3. Harry Emerson Fosdick, *The Secret of Victorious Living* (New York: Harper & Bros., 1934), pp. 117–19.

4. Mark Guy Pearse, "Pardoning Grace, Then Honor," *2500 Best Modern Illustrations*, ed. G. B. F. Hallock (New York: Harper & Bros., 1935), p. 261.